Wil.

Series

OLD TESTAMENT STORIES

Roy Wilkinson

RSCP

The publisher is grateful for the encouragement and support of Robert Dulaney in making this new edition possible.

The name Waldorf really belongs only to the first school of its type, the one founded by Rudolf Steiner in Stuttgart, Germany for the children of the workers at the Waldorf-Astoria factory. It has since been adopted as the generic name of schools conducted according to Rudolf Steiner's recommendations. In place of Waldorf some establishments call themselves Rudolf Steiner schools. Others take a distinctive name and add Waldorf or Rudolf Steiner in some connection as a subtitle.

Revised 2002

ISBN 0-945803-59-1

Book orders may be made through Rudolf Steiner College Bookstore. Tel: 916-961-8729, FAX: 916-961-3032, E-mail: www.steinercollege.edu.

Rudolf Steiner College Press
9200 Fair Oaks Blvd.
Fair Oaks, CA 95628, U.S.A.

Table of Contents

Introduction

The stories in this book are taken from that part of the Bible known as the Old Testament, the greater part of which was written in Hebrew, a language very different from our own. When translating from one language to another, it is very difficult to reproduce the exact meaning and it is therefore possible to have translations which differ from one another.

Although, for the most part, the stories presented here are based on the authorised English [King James] translation of the Bible in common use throughout the English-speaking world, there are several points to which reference should be made. In the authorised version we read about God, the Lord God, and the Lord. The Hebrew equivalents are: Elohim, Jehovah Elohim, and Jehovah. These terms have been used in this book. Elohim is the name of heavenly beings of high rank. It is a plural form, i.e. gods. Jehovah Elohim was one of their number who had a special mission in connection with the earth. He was often referred to simply as Jehovah.

Some of the most impressive words in the Old Testament are to be found in the opening chapter, the story of creation. Two versions of this story are given here. The first is from the authorised version of the Bible; no attempt has been made to deal with the question of gender. The second version is based on the author's interpretation of suggestions concerning the stories made by the Austrian philosopher and scholar, Rudolf Steiner, to whom we are indebted for clarification of other passages.

In the schools that follow the indications of Rudolf Steiner, a sequence of stories is given, related to the stages of human development. They are a form of spiritual nourishment.

In the early years, fairy stories provide suitable material, followed by fables and legends. At the age of nine or ten, Old Testament stories are recommended; in subsequent years, Norse and Greek mythologies. The Old Testament stories should first be told by the teacher, then read by the children. It is to be hoped that this book provides both suitable guidance for the teacher and suitable reading material for the child.

Dr. Steiner points out that it is educationally inadequate if a teacher merely tells such stories as these. They have a deep significance which teachers must carry in their souls so that their words actually convey more than they say, without, of course, pointing any morals or giving explanations. For such teachers, and parents and anyone else interested, the author has written a companion volume, *Commentary on Old Testament Stories,* giving more detailed interpretation based on Rudolf Steiner's writings and lectures.

THE SEVEN DAYS OF CREATION

From the authorised version of the Bible

In the beginning God created the heaven and the earth. And the earth was without form and void; and darkness was upon the face of the deep. And the Spirit of God moved upon the face of the waters.

And God said, Let there be light: and there was light. And God saw the light that it was good: and God divided the light from the darkness. And God called the light Day, and the darkness he called Night. And the evening and the morning were the first day.

And God said, Let there be a firmament in the midst of the waters, and let it divide the waters from the waters. And God made the firmament, and divided the waters which were under the firmament from the waters which were above the firmament: and it was so. And God called the firmament Heaven. And the evening and the morning were the second day.

And God said, Let the waters under the heaven be gathered together unto one place, and let the dry land appear: and it was so. And God called the dry land Earth; and the gathering together of the waters called he Seas: and God saw that it was good. And God said, Let the earth bring forth grass, the herb yielding seed, and the fruit tree yielding fruit after his kind, whose seed is in itself, upon the earth: and it was so: and God saw that it was good. And the evening and the morning were the third day.

And God said, Let there be lights in the firmament of the heaven to divide the day from the night; and let them be for signs and for seasons, and for days, and years: and let them be for lights in the firmament of the heaven to give light upon the earth: and it was so. And God made two great lights; the greater light to rule the day, and the lesser light to rule the night: he made the stars also. And God set them in the firmament of the heaven to give light upon the earth, and to rule over the day and over the night, and to divide the light from the darkness: and God saw that it was good. And the evening and the morning were the fourth day.

And God said, Let the waters bring forth abundantly the moving creature that hath life, and fowl that may fly above the earth in the open firmament of heaven. And God created great whales, and every living creature that moveth, which the waters brought forth abundantly, after their kind, and every winged fowl after his kind: and God saw that it was good. And God blessed them, saying, Be fruitful, and multiply, and fill the waters in the seas, and let fowl multiply in the earth. And the evening and the morning were the fifth day.

And God said, Let the earth bring forth the living creature after his kind, cattle, and creeping thing, and beast of the earth after his kind: and it was so. And God made the beast of the earth after his kind, and cattle after their kind, and everything that creepeth upon the earth after his kind: and God saw that it was good. And God said, Let us make man in our image, after our likeness: and let them have dominion over the fish of the sea, and over the fowl of the air, and over the cattle, and over all the earth. So God created man in his own image, in the image of God created he him, male and female created he them. And God blessed them and said, Be fruitful and multiply. Behold, I have given you every herb-bearing seed and every tree; to you it shall be for meat. And God saw everything that he had made, and, behold, it was very good. And the evening and the morning were the sixth day.

Thus the heavens and the earth were finished. And on the seventh day God ended his work which he had made; and he rested on the seventh day from all his work which he had made.

EARTH: ITS CREATORS
AND FIRST INHABITANTS
From the creation of the earth to its consolidation

THE SEVEN DAYS OF CREATION

Before there was earth, or plants, or trees or animals, or human beings, there were heavenly beings; and the heavenly beings gave of their substance that the sun, moon, planets, the earth with all its inhabitants, might be created.

In the wide spaces of the universe, amid the stars, these heavenly beings formed a huge sphere of warm, cloud-like substance in which they dwelt. Time was non-existent; neither was material shape or form. Darkness prevailed.

Seven Spirits of Form, of the hierarchy of the Elohim, conceived in their minds a great project—human beings, creatures both greater and lesser than themselves, doers and thinkers, within a universe. Possessed of divine power, their vision took shape and the fashioning of the earth, and an earthly form for humans, began.

All these things lived first in the minds of the Elohim.

Into the darkness of the great sphere the Elohim spoke: "Let there be light." The power of their words transformed the substance. Light and air were born. To sustain the light they brought forth from themselves spirits of light as servants, and the spirits of light were given alternate rule with the spirits of darkness.

The Elohim uttered their further thoughts: "Let there be a firmament in the midst of the waters." In the air a light mist floated upwards and a heavier watery element sank down. Between the two was the firmament.

Again the Elohim spoke: "Let the waters be gathered into one place and let the dry land appear." The waters gathered slowly together and were called seas. Land appeared and slowly it dried out. Yet again the Elohim spoke: "Let spirit forms of plants and trees be over the land," and it was so.

By the work of the Elohim the nature of the great sphere was changed and thereby certain of its inhabitants left. They created sun, moon, and planets for their habitations and radiated their power to earth from outside. Heavenly beings set the orbs in the firmament on their courses so that they moved among the stars in harmony and fixed procession.

The Elohim spoke again: "Let there be living creatures in water and in air. Let them be fruitful and multiply." Thus souls of fish and fowl were made. "Let there be living creatures on the land," said the Elohim, and souls of land animals appeared.

The Elohim then said: "Let us make a human being in our own image," and they made a human form in their own likeness, neither male nor female, but both in one.

Still there was no firm earth, and the human being was not made of flesh.

To sustain their creation the Elohim brought forth from themselves descendants as servants. Thus, besides the spirits of light, they created beings to live in earth, water, air, and fire.

Now that this stage of creation was reached, the Elohim divided their strength. Six of them had other tasks, but the six bestowed special gifts on the seventh that he might especially further their work on the earth. His name was Jehovah, or, showing to which rank he belonged, Jehovah Elohim. To fit the human being for life on earth, Jehovah Elohim now used earthly forces to reshape the human form and he breathed into it and the human spirit came down from heavenly heights to live in it.

THE GARDEN OF EDEN

Earth was not yet ready for man. Heavenly beings worked with Jehovah Elohim to make it a suitable dwelling place for him. They firmed its substances. They brought down the spirit forms of plants to grow in the soil. They brought down the souls of animals to live in earthly bodies. But the spirit of the human being which the Elohim had conceived still lived in heavenly regions.

Jehovah Elohim now prepared a special dwelling place for the human being whom he had made. It was in a heavenly region called Paradise and the name thereof was the Garden of Eden. There he put the human being whom he named Adam. Adam means 'Earth Being.'

The garden had heavenly plants and trees and Jehovah Elohim commanded Adam, saying, "Of every tree in the garden thou mayest freely eat, but of the tree of the knowledge of good and evil, thou shalt not eat of it; for in the day that thou eatest thereof, thou shalt surely die."

Jehovah Elohim also reshaped the animal forms with earthly forces and brought them to Adam to receive a name.

Jehovah Elohim saw that Adam was lonely. He therefore created another, different, human being, with a different form, a woman. When this happened, Adam's nature changed. He felt his manhood. His companion was called Eve.

They lived happily together in Paradise and should have stayed there a long time but the Evil One conspired to get them out early. His name was Lucifer.

ADAM AND EVE ARE EXPELLED FROM PARADISE

Lucifer was a great and mighty angelic being who had become proud and wanted to rule in heaven; hence he was cast forth from among his peers. He did not know that it was Jehovah Elohim who had made the Garden of Eden and put human beings in it. He took on the shape of a serpent and came to Eve, saying, "Have not the Elohim said that you may eat of the fruit of every tree in the garden?" and Eve answered, "We may eat of every tree save the one that is in the midst. If we eat of that, we die." "Nay," said the serpent, "you will not die; your eyes will be opened and you will be like gods, knowing good and evil."

The woman looked, saw that the fruit was good, and ate thereof. She gave some to Adam and he ate it. They looked around. They noticed that they were naked and the world was changed. They were afraid and hid.

Jehovah Elohim came and called to Adam: "Where art thou? Hast thou eaten of the fruit that I forbade thee?"

Adam was shame-faced and confessed with a heavy heart. Jehovah Elohim turned to the woman and said, "In sorrow shalt thou now bring forth children." To Adam he said, "Now must thou earn thy bread in the sweat of thy face," and to both, "Now you must leave this heavenly place." So Adam and Eve were driven forth to live on earth where their spirits were clothed with earthly bodies and where they would meet sickness and death.

To guard the gates of Paradise, Jehovah Elohim set Cherubim with flaming swords.

[*In the course of time, less mention was made of the Elohim, the heavenly creators, although they still took part in earth's affairs. The fact that Jehovah was one of the Elohim was overlooked and he was referred to simply as Jehovah. The Jewish people who were true to their faith looked upon Jehovah as their special god and as the Father-Creator of the world.*]

CAIN AND ABEL

Time passed and Eve bore a son whose name was Cain. The way of life on earth was different from that in Paradise, and many changes took place in the earth itself.

Eve bore another son, Abel, and Abel differed much from his brother. Cain became a tiller of the ground and knew not the difference between good and evil. Abel was a keeper of sheep and righteous.

It came to pass that Cain brought produce of his labour in the field as an offering to Jehovah, and Abel brought one of his lambs. Jehovah was pleased with Abel and his gift, but from Cain he turned away because his was an unworthy offering. Cain was very wroth and his face fell but Jehovah spoke to him, saying, "Cain, why art thou wroth? If what thou doest is good, I shall be pleased. It lies within thy power to do what is right." But Cain did not understand and his heart was full of jealousy and anger. He talked with his brother in the field, rose up against him and slew him.

Then Jehovah spoke to Cain, saying, "Cain, where is Abel, thy brother?" and Cain answered, "I know not, am I my brother's keeper?" Jehovah spoke again: "What hast thou done? The voice of thy brother's blood is calling to me from the ground and now thou art cursed from the earth which has opened her mouth to receive thy brother's blood from thy hand. Henceforth when thou tillest the ground, it shall not yield unto thee her strength as before. A fugitive and a vagabond shalt thou be on earth."

In fear Cain answered, "Guilt like mine is too great to find forgiveness. From thy face shall I now be hid and anyone that finds me will slay me." But Jehovah put a mark on Cain as a sign and as a warning that he should not be harmed, for Cain now recognised his transgression and knew that he must make amends.

So Cain went out from the presence of Jehovah and away from his own country. In a strange land a son was born to him and his wife. He called the boy Enoch and he built a city, giving it the self-same name.

The city which Cain built became great by reason of the wisdom and knowledge of its inhabitants and Cain's descendants became cunning craftsmen; some raised cattle, others made harps and organs, yet others were workers in brass and iron. Abel was the first person on earth to be killed. After his death, Eve had another son, whom, she said, had been appointed to her in place of Abel; and this son, Seth, became one of the world's wise men.

NOAH AND THE FLOOD

Many people now lived upon the earth and some of them were giants. It came to pass that their wickedness became great, the thoughts of their hearts were evil, and the earth was corrupted. The Elohim, the heavenly beings who had created the earth, saw this and resolved that it must be cleansed. Jehovah grieved that he had made Adam.

There was, howbeit, one just and perfect man whose name was Noah. When the Elohim decided to cleanse the earth, they spoke to Noah, saying, "Through people the earth is corrupt and filled with violence. Behold, we will destroy both earth and its inhabitants. Make thee an ark of gopher wood with rooms sealed inside and out with pitch. The length of the ark shall be three hundred cubits, the breadth of it fifty cubits; and the height, thirty cubits. Make a window at the top and a door at the side and it shall have three storeys. We shall bring a flood of waters on the earth and everything that is on the earth shall die, but with thee will we establish a covenant. Thou shalt come into the ark, thou, and thy sons, and thy wife, and thy sons' wives with thee. Of every living thing shalt thou bring into the ark two of every sort, male and female. Take also food for thee and for them."

Thus Noah did according to all that the Elohim commanded him. When the ark was finished, Jehovah said to Noah, "Come now, and all thy house into the ark. In seven days' time it will rain upon the earth and it will not cease for forty days and forty nights." So Noah went in with all his family. Of every living thing of flesh there went in two and two also into the ark.

When the seven days had passed, the fountains of the great deep were set free and the windows of heaven were opened. It rained upon the earth for forty days and forty nights. The waters increased and bore up the ark above the earth and the ark floated on the surface of the waters. Hills and mountains disappeared under the covering of the waters.

After one hundred and fifty days the Elohim made a warm wind to blow. The rain from heaven was restrained and the waters abated. In the seventh month, on the seventeenth day of the month, the ark rested on the mountains of Ararat.

At the end of forty days Noah opened the window of the ark and sent forth a raven which went to and fro until the waters were dried up from off the earth. Also he sent forth a dove, but the dove found no place to rest and returned to him again. He stayed yet seven days and again sent forth the dove. In the evening she returned to him and lo, in her mouth was an olive leaf. So Noah knew that the waters were abated from the face of the earth. He stayed yet another seven days and sent forth the dove again, but this time she returned to him no more. Then Noah removed the covering of the ark and looked; and behold, the face of the earth was dry.

Then the Elohim spoke to Noah, saying, "Go forth from the ark, thou and thy wife, thy sons and thy sons' wives with thee. Bring forth every living thing that is with thee that they may breed and be fruitful and multiply upon the earth."

So all who had sojourned in the ark went forth and Noah built an altar and gave thanks for his deliverance. Jehovah was pleased and said in his heart, "The ground shall never again be cursed or living things destroyed because of human beings. As long as the earth exists, seed time and harvest, cold and heat, summer and winter, day and night, shall not cease."

Then the Elohim blessed Noah and his sons and said to them, "Be fruitful and multiply, replenish the earth and let no man shed another's blood. We will establish a covenant with you. Waters of a flood shall never again destroy the earth. Behold now, we do set our bow in the cloud and it shall be for a token of the covenant between us and the earth. When we bring a cloud over the earth, the rainbow shall be seen in the cloud and we shall remember our covenant. The waters shall no more become a flood to destroy the earth."

So the land dried out and was ready to be tilled. Noah became a husbandman. He planted a vineyard and drank of the wine. He became drunk and lay naked in his dwelling. One of his sons, Ham, saw him and made fun of him but the other brothers protested and covered their father with a garment.

Now the names of Noah's sons were Shem, Ham and Japhet and when these three were grown up, they went out into the world and became the fathers of different peoples. Some of the descendants of Ham settled in the land of Canaan and the descendants of Shem fought wars with them to possess it.

At that time there was one language throughout the earth. The descendants of Noah came from the east to the plain of Shinar and dwelt there. They said to one another, "Let us make bricks and build ourselves a city and a tower whose top may reach unto heaven and let us make a name for ourselves."

Jehovah came down to see the city and the tower and said, "Behold the people are one; they have all one language and now they act foolishly. Let us go down and there confound their language that they may not understand one another's speech" So Jehovah scattered them abroad upon the face of all the earth and they left off to build the city. Therefore is the name of the place called Babel, which, being interpreted, means 'The Gate of God' because Jehovah did there confound the language and scatter the people.

FOUNDERS OF THE ISRAELITE NATION

The Patriarchs: Abraham, Isaac, Jacob

THE PROMISED LAND

In the land which was once known as the Plain of Shinar was built a great city called Ur, or Ur of the Chaldees, after the wise men who lived there.

From this city a certain man, named Terah, journeyed north to live in another great city called Haran. With him went his son, Abram, Abram's wife, Lot (a son of Abram's brother), and Lot's wife. In Haran Terah died.

Now Abram was a wise and learned man and after the death of Terah, Jehovah spoke to him, saying, "Get thee forth from this country and from thy kindred and from thy father's house unto a land that I will show thee. I will make of thee a great nation and thy seed shall be in numbers as the stars of heaven."

So Abram departed as Jehovah had commanded him; and he took Sarah, his wife, Lot, his brother's son, and all the servants and substance they had, and went forth into the land of Canaan. When they came there, they found grievous famine in the land so they journeyed south into Egypt until the time of famine was past.

When Abram returned to Canaan, he had become very rich in cattle, in silver and in gold. Lot, also, who went with him, had flocks and herds and tents. Their substance was so great that the land was not able to bear them both and they could not dwell together. The herdmen of Abram's cattle and the herdmen of Lot's cattle quarrelled with one another; but Abram said unto Lot, "Let there be no strife, I pray thee, between me and thee, and between my herdmen and thy herdmen, for we are brethren. Is not the whole world before us? Separate thyself, I pray thee, from me; if thou wilt take the left hand, then I will go to the right; or if thou depart to the right hand, then I will go to the left." Then Lot chose the well-watered plain of Jordan and took his way east towards Sodom. This was before Sodom was destroyed for its wickedness.

Jehovah then said to Abram, after Lot had separated from him, "Lift up now thine eyes and look from the place where thou art, northward, and southward, and eastward, and westward, for all the land that thou seest, to thee will I give it and to thy seed for ever. Arise, walk through the land in the length of it and in the breadth of it." Then Abram came and dwelt in the plain of Mamre, which is in Hebron, and built an altar to Jehovah.

Now it came to pass that certain kings made war on the king of Sodom and they took away Lot and all his possessions. When Abram heard that his brother's son had been taken captive, he armed his trained servants and went forth to rescue him and he brought back Lot and all his goods.

As he was returning to his own place, a certain wise and mighty man, Melchizedek, King of Salem, and a priest of the Most High God, came to meet him. Melchizedek greeted Abram, set bread and wine before him and blessed him; and when Abram was refreshed, he journeyed homeward rejoicing.

When Abram was nine-and-ninety years old, Jehovah appeared to him and spoke to him, saying, "I am the Almighty God; walk before me and be thou perfect," and the Elohim continued: "Henceforth thy name shall not be Abram but Abraham, for a father of many peoples shalt thou be. We will establish a covenant with thee and with thy seed after thee; and to thee and to thy seed shall be given the land of Canaan for an everlasting possession. As for Sarah, thy wife, she will be blessed and will bear a son and thou shalt call his name Isaac."

Abraham rejoiced but wondered in his heart that a child should be born to him and his wife in their old age.

ABRAHAM ENTERTAINS VISITORS

One day, Abraham sat in the doorway of his dwelling in the heat of the day and he lifted up his eyes and looked; and lo, three figures in the form of men stood before him; and when he saw them, he ran to meet them and bowed himself towards the ground and said to the most exalted of them. "My Lord, if now I have found favor in thy sight, pass not away, I pray thee, from thy servant." Then he addressed all three: "Let a little water be fetched, I pray you, and wash your feet and rest yourselves under the tree. I will fetch a morsel of bread to comfort you. After that you shall proceed," and they answered, "So do, as thou hast said."

So Abraham hastened into his dwelling and told Sarah to make ready quickly three measures of fine meal, to knead it, and to make cakes, and to prepare food and drink. When the guests had finished their meal, the chief of the three said to Abraham, "I will return in due season when Sarah, thy wife, shall have had her son."

THE WICKED CITIES OF SODOM AND GOMORRHA

Then the three departed towards Sodom, and Abraham went with them to bring them on the way; and Abraham perceived that his guests were Jehovah and two angels. The two journeyed on but Jehovah tarried to speak privily with Abraham, saying, "The sins of the people of Sodom are great. I will go down and judge them." But Abraham asked, "Wilt thou also destroy the righteous with the wicked? Peradventure there be fifty righteous within the city," and Jehovah said, "If I find fifty righteous within the city, then I will spare all the place for their sakes." Abraham spoke again: "Peradventure there shall lack five of the fifty righteous. Wilt thou destroy all the city for the lack of five?" and Jehovah answered, "If I find there forty and five, I will not destroy it." Yet again Abraham spoke to Jehovah and said, "Peradventure there shall be forty found there," and Jehovah replied, "I will not do it for forty's sake." Again Abraham spoke: "O let not my Lord be angry. Peradventure there shall be thirty found there," and Jehovah said, "I will not do it if I find thirty there." Once more Abraham spoke unto Jehovah: "Peradventure there shall be twenty found there," and Jehovah answered, "I will not do it for twenty's sake." Again Abraham said, "O let not my Lord be angry and I will speak but yet this once: peradventure ten righteous persons shall be found there," and Jehovah replied, "I will not destroy it for ten's sake." Then he went on his way and Abraham returned unto his place.

ANGELS VISIT ABRAHAM'S NEPHEW

But there lived not even ten righteous persons in Sodom, only Lot, Abraham's brother's son. At eventide, the two angels, in the guise of men, came to Sodom; and Lot, sitting by the city gate, rose to meet them. He bowed towards them and said, "Behold now, turn in, I pray you, to your servant's house; tarry all night, wash your feet, and you shall rise up early and go on your way."

But the people of Sodom called to Lot demanding to know who the strangers were and they came near to breaking the door of his dwelling. Then the angels struck the people at the door with blindness so that they knew not where they were.

THE DESTRUCTION OF SODOM AND GOMORRAH

When morning came, the two angels hastened Lot, saying, "Arise, take thy wife and thy two daughters lest thou be consumed in the wickedness of this city." They took his hand and the hands of his daughters and brought them forth outside the city and then said to Lot, "Escape for thy life; look not behind thee; neither stay thou in all the plain; escape to the mountain lest thou be consumed." So Lot and his wife and his children ran towards the mountain as brimstone and fire out of heaven rained down upon Sodom and Gomorrah, but Lot's wife looked back and she was turned into a pillar of salt.

Then were those cities destroyed, together with all the plain, and all the inhabitants thereof.

As the Elohim had foretold, Sarah bore a son in due season, and Abraham called his name Isaac.

It came to pass after these things that the Elohim desired to prove Abraham, whether his spirit was steadfast in their service. They said to him, "Abraham, take now thy son whom thou lovest and get thee into the land of Moriah. Offer him there for a burnt offering upon the mountain."

Abraham rose up early in the morning, saddled his ass, took two of his young men with him, and Isaac, his son. He took chopped wood for the burnt offering and went forth. On the third day he lifted up his eyes and saw the mountain afar off. He said unto his young men, "Abide ye here with the ass; I and the lad will go yonder and worship." He took the wood and laid it upon his son. He took the fire in his hand and a knife, and they went both of them together.

Isaac then spoke to Abraham and said, "My father, behold the fire and the wood, but where is the lamb for the burnt offering?" and Abraham answered, "My son, the Elohim will provide."

They came to the mountain and Abraham built an altar there, laid the wood in order, bound Isaac, and laid him on the wood. He raised the knife and Isaac's soul fled; but the Archangel Michael, the servant of Jehovah, called to Abraham out of heaven, saying, "Abraham, Abraham, lay not thine hand upon the lad. Thou hast proved thyself a god-fearing man, seeing thou hast not withheld thy son, thine only son," and the lad's soul returned unto his body and he awoke.

Abraham lifted up his eyes and saw a ram caught in a thicket by his horns. So Abraham took the ram and offered him up in the place of his son.

Then the angel called unto Abraham a second time out of heaven and said, "Thus says Jehovah: because thou wouldst offer up thy son and not withhold him and thou hast proved thyself, I will bless thee and multiply thy seed as the stars in heaven and as the sand upon the sea shore; and in thy seed shall all nations of the earth be blessed."

So Abraham returned unto his young men, and they rose up and went together to Beersheba, and Abraham dwelt there.

ISAAC AND REBEKAH

Abraham grew old and Jehovah had blessed him in all things. One day, Abraham said to the eldest servant of his household, "Go thou now to my country and to my kindred and seek there a wife for my son, Isaac." But the servant replied, "Peradventure the maiden is not willing to follow me into this land." Abraham answered, "Jehovah Elohim instructed me. He will send his angel before thee and thou wilt find a wife for my son."

The servant took ten camels and departed. He went to the city of Haran where Nahor, Abraham's brother, lived. At eventide, he approached the city and made his camels kneel down by a well at the hour when the women would come out to fetch water. There he said to himself, "O Lord God of my master, Abraham, show kindness to my master. Behold, I stand here by the well and the women of the city come out to draw water. Let it come to pass that the damsel to whom I shall say: let down thy pitcher, I pray thee, that I may drink;—and she shall say: drink and thy camels also;—let the same be she that thou has appointed for thy servant, Isaac."

Before he had done speaking, a damsel came out with a pitcher on her shoulder. She was very fair to look upon and she came to the well and filled her pitcher. The servant said to her, "Let me, I pray thee, drink a little water from thy pitcher." "Drink, sire," she answered, "and I will draw water for thy camels also." She hastened and emptied her pitcher into the drinking trough and ran again to the well to draw water for all the camels. The man, wondering at her, held his peace until the camels had done drinking. Then he took a golden earring and two bracelets of gold from his store and gave them to the maiden, asking, "Whose daughter art thou? What is thy name? Tell me, pray thee, if there is room in thy father's house for us to lodge."

The damsel answered, "I am the daughter of Bethuel, son of Milcar and Nahor, who is the brother of Abraham. I am called

Rebekah. We have both food and straw enough and room for you to lodge." Then the man bowed his head, saying, "Blessed be the Lord God of my master, Abraham, who has led me to the house of my master's brethren."

Now Rebekah had a brother whose name was Laban. He ran out to the well and called to Abraham's servant: "Come in, thou blessed of Jehovah. I have prepared the house and have room for the camels also."

A meal was set before the guest but he would not eat until he had explained his errand. Thereupon he spoke of his master's desires, of his journey, and of his meeting with Rebekah at the well.

Then Laban and Bethuel said, "This thing proceeds from Jehovah. Behold, Rebekah is before thee; take her and go; and let her be the wife of thy master's son as Jehovah has ordained."

When Abraham's servant heard these words, he bowed himself to the earth and rejoiced greatly. He brought forth jewels of silver, jewels of gold, and raiment, and gave them to Rebekah. He gave also precious things to her brother and to her mother. He joined in the feast and tarried the night. When morning was come, he made ready to depart but Rebekah's mother and brother spoke, saying, "We will call the damsel and enquire if she is willing to go with thee." So they called Rebekah and Rebekah replied, "Certainly, I will go." whereupon her mother and her brother gave her their blessing.

So Rebekah and her maidservants rode away on the camels which Abraham's servant had brought with him.

Now Isaac had been sitting by the well of Lahai-roi, which means 'of the living and seeing,' and he went out at eventide to meditate in the field. Lifting up his eyes, he saw camels approaching and a fair damsel riding on one of them. Rebekah, seeing Isaac and understanding that this was her future husband, alighted from her camel and put a veil before her face; and Isaac went forth to meet her and led her into his mother's dwelling. In due season he took her to wife and loved her exceedingly.

ISAAC DIGS WELLS AND MAKES THE LAND FRUITFUL

When these things were fulfilled, Abraham gave all that he had to Isaac and died in the fullness of years. He was buried near Mamre, in Hebron, where he had once built an altar. Sarah, Abraham's wife, who had died earlier, was also buried there.

As in the time of Abraham, it came to pass that there was famine in the land and the word of Jehovah came to Isaac, saying, "Go not down into Egypt but sojourn in a land which I will show thee." So Isaac dwelt in Gerar, sowed in that land and received in the same year a hundredfold. Jehovah blessed him and he had possession of flocks, of herds, and a great store of servants. There had been many wells in that land dug by Abraham and his servants but the Philistines had stopped them up and filled them with earth. Now Isaac ordered his servants to open up the wells again, and the land became fruitful.

Isaac became rich and the Philistines were envious. Their king spoke to Isaac, saying, "Thou are become much mightier than we. I pray thee, therefore, go now from us."

So Isaac departed and dwelt some way off in the valley of Gerar. There he opened the wells of water which had been dug in the days of his father, Abraham, and which the Philistines had stopped up.

Then there was strife over them between the herdmen of Gerar and Isaac's herdmen, so Isaac dug more wells further off, over which there was no strife, and said, "The Lord has made room for us all and we shall be fruitful in the land."

Time passed and Isaac went to dwell in Beersheba where he ordered his servants to dig wells also. Then he journeyed to Mamre where he died.

TWINS ARE BORN TO ISAAC: ESAU AND JACOB

Isaac was forty years old when he took Rebekah to wife and they dwelt together childless for thirty years. Then Isaac entreated heaven for his wife and for himself, and Jehovah made promise that in due season twin boys would be born to them. To Rebekah herself Jehovah vouchsafed that the boys would differ from one another exceedingly and that the elder would have to serve the younger. When the twins were born, the first to appear had a red skin and was called Esau. The second was named Jacob and, at the birth, Jacob had hold of his brother's heel.

The twins grew to be men and Esau became a hunter and a man of the field, but Jacob liked to stay in his dwelling. Isaac loved Esau because he brought him venison, but Rebekah loved Jacob.

ESAU SELLS HIS BIRTHRIGHT

One day, Jacob was making a broth when Esau came to him, saying, "Feed me, I pray you, for I am faint with hunger." Jacob was cleverer than his brother and he answered, "Let us make an exchange. Yield to me your birthright, your right of inheritance as the first-born, and I will give you broth." "If I am about to die," replied Esau, "how shall the inheritance profit me?" and he sold his birthright to Jacob for bread and broth and went away. Thus he showed no concern for the future.

Isaac grew old and his eyes were dim so that he could not see. Feeling his age, he called Esau and said to him, "My son, behold now, I am old and know not the day of my death. Now therefore take, I pray thee, thy quiver and thy bow and find me some venison. Make me savory meat such as I love, that I may eat and that my soul may bless thee and I may bestow on thee the inheritance before I die." Therefore Esau went to the field to hunt venison.

Now Rebekah heard what Isaac said to Esau, and she remembered what Jehovah had told her, that the elder must serve the younger, and she knew secretly in her heart that it was ordained for Jacob to receive the inheritance. She therefore spoke to Jacob, saying, "Go now to the flocks and bring me two good kids and I will make them savory meat for thy father, such as he loves, and thou shalt bring it to thy father and thou shalt be given the inheritance with his blessing." But Jacob answered, "Behold, Esau, my brother, is a hairy man and my skin is smooth. My father will per-adventure feel me and curse me," but Rebekah only said, "Obey my voice; fetch the meat; any curse will fall on me."

When it was prepared, Rebekah took goodly raiment of her eldest son and put it on Jacob, and she put the skins of the kids on his hands and on the smooth of his neck.

Thus Jacob came to his father with the savory meat and Isaac ate it, blessed him and apportioned him the birthright.

When Jacob had scarcely gone from the presence of his father, Esau came in with his dish of meat, saying, "Let my father now eat of his son's venison that thy soul may bless me." Isaac was surprised and asked, "Who art thou?" and Esau answered, "I am Esau, thy first-born."

Then Isaac trembled exceedingly and could scarcely find speech. He murmured: "My son, there came one before thee whom I supposed was thee—Jacob, in thy guise. Now I have made him foremost. Thy brother have I made master of the household and of thee and on him have I bestowed the birthright. I cannot withdraw it and it must remain so. Yet it will come about that thou shalt become strong and break his yoke from off thy neck."

At these words Esau grew angry and hated his brother. He thought to himself, "The days of my father are numbered and when he is dead, I will slay Jacob," but Rebekah knew what was in his heart. She called Jacob and said to him, "Behold, thy broth-er, Esau, means to kill thee. Therefore, my son, arise and flee to Laban, my brother in Haran, and remain with him until thy brother's fury shall turn away. Then I will send for thee."

JACOB FLEES. HE HAS A VISION OF ANGELS ASCENDING AND DESCENDING A LADDER TO HEAVEN

So Jacob prepared to leave his father's house but before he went, he sought out Isaac, his father, to say farewell; and Isaac blessed him and exhorted him to seek a wife while he was away.

Jacob set forth towards Haran and he came to a certain place where he decided to stay the night because the sun had set. He took of the stones of that place for his pillow and lay down to sleep. He dreamed and beheld a ladder set up on the earth whose top reached to heaven, and angels were ascending and descending upon it. Jehovah stood above it and said to Jacob, "I am Jehovah Elohim, the Lord God of Abraham and Isaac. The land whereon thou liest, to thee will I give it and to thy seed. I am with thee and will keep thee in all places whither thou goest."

Jacob awoke out of his sleep murmuring: "Surely Jehovah is in this place and I knew it not." He rose up early in the morning and he took the stone on which his head had rested and he set it up as a pillar, and he called the place Bethel which means 'House of God.'

THE MEETING AT THE WELL.
JACOB TAKES SERVICE WITH HIS UNCLE LABAN

Then he journeyed further and came into the land of the people of the east, and he saw a well in a field and three flocks of sheep lying beside it. He spoke to the shepherds there, saying, "My brethren, know ye Laban, son of Nahor?" and they answered, "Certainly we know him. Look yonder and thou wilt see Rachel, his daughter, coming to the well with her father's sheep."

When Rachel reached the well with her father's flocks, Jacob drew water for them. He kissed Rachel and made himself known to her as the son of Rebekah, her father's sister, and she ran home quickly to tell her father, who then came to meet the visitor. He embraced Jacob and brought him into his house.

Now Laban had two daughters. The name of the elder was Leah, and the younger was Rachel. Jacob loved Rachel and said to Laban, "I will serve thee seven years for Rachel, thy younger daughter," and Jacob served for seven years but they seemed only days because of the love he felt.

The time came when the seven years were fulfilled and Jacob addressed Laban: "Give me now my wife, I pray thee, for I have served my time," but Laban brought Leah to Jacob who, some-what astonished, said, "Did I not serve thee for Rachel?" but Laban replied, "It is not custom in our country to give the younger before the first-born. Take therefore Leah, and Rachel will I also give thee in return for a further seven years' service."

So Jacob stayed with Laban and in all he abode with him twenty years. He served also six years for a share of flocks and cattle and he became rich.

DISPUTE AND RECONCILIATION

But there arose strife between Laban and Jacob regarding wages and the word of Jehovah came to Jacob, saying, "Return to the land of thy fathers and I will be with thee."

So Jacob took his wives and his children, and his menservants, and maidservants, and all his flocks and cattle, and goods, and rode away from Haran; and Laban knew it not. When he was informed, he followed after Jacob and overtook him but on the way the Elohim warned Laban: "Take heed how thou speakest to Jacob."

When they came together, Laban asked Jacob, "Why hast thou stolen away unawares to me and carried away my daughters without my farewell and why hast thou stolen my gods?" Jacob answered, "I have stolen none of thy goods and none of thy gods," but he did not know that Rachel had taken some of her father's images and was sitting on them on the camel. He grew angry and said, ""I have served thee fourteen years for thy two daughters and six years for the cattle. Thou hast changed my wages ten times and had not the God of Abraham and Isaac been with me, surely thou wouldst have sent me away empty. It was revealed to me that yesternight the Elohim spoke to thee and rebuked thee."

Then Laban repented and was pacified and he replied gently, "Let there be no strife between us but let us make a covenant that there be peace."

Jacob took up a stone and set it up for a pillar and ordered his men to gather more stones to make a heap. Laban also erected a pillar. Then they ate bread together on the heap and early in the morning Laban rose up, kissed his sons and his daughters, blessed them, and returned to his own place.

A MESSAGE TO ESAU

Jacob also went on his way and angels met him. The place where he met them he called Mahanaim which means 'God's host.' Then he sent messengers to his brother, Esau, and he commanded them to say to him, "Thy servant, Jacob, speaks thus: I have sojourned with Laban and stayed there until now. I have oxen, asses, flocks, menservants, maidservants. I have sent to tell thee of my return that I may find grace in thy sight."

The messengers sought out Esau, delivered the message and returned to Jacob with the words: "We came to thy brother, Esau. He is coming to meet thee and four hundred men with him."

Then Jacob sent a present of many goats, sheep, camels, foals and cattle to his brother and sat down to await his coming.

JACOB WRESTLES WITH AN ANGEL

In the night a figure in the likeness of a man came to Jacob and wrestled with him and the struggle ceased not until daybreak. When the man saw that he could not prevail, he touched the hollow of Jacob's thigh and put it out of joint. Then he cried: "Let me go for the day is breaking," but Jacob replied, "I will not let thee go unless thou bless me." The man asked, "What is thy name?" and Jacob answered with his name. "Henceforth," said the man, "thou shalt be called Israel, which means 'He who wrestled with an angel,' for thou hast been tested by the Elohim and found worthy. As a prince hast thou power with spirits and with humans." (Therefore are the children of Jacob, his grandchildren and the children after them called the Children of Israel or the Israelites.) The angel, for such he was, blessed Jacob, and Jacob called the place Peniel, which means 'I have seen heavenly beings face to face.

The next morning Esau came with four hundred men. Jacob went to meet him bowing to the ground but Esau ran to him, embraced him and kissed him; and they both wept. Then Esau asked the meaning of the flocks and cattle which had been sent to him and said, "I have enough, my brother; keep what thou hast for thyself." But Jacob urged him to take the present and his blessing with it, and Esau did so.

Thus Jacob returned to Canaan, to the city of Shalem, where he bought a piece of land and built an altar.

He journeyed also to Mamre, in Hebron, to his father, Isaac, who was now very old and full of days; and when Isaac died, his sons Esau and Jacob buried him.

THE STORY OF JOB

Trials, troubles and faith

JOB KEEPS FAITH THROUGH ALL HIS AFFLICTIONS

At the time of the Patriarchs there lived a man in the land of Uz whose name was Job. He was a perfect, upright, god-fearing man who shunned evil. There were born to him seven sons and three daughters. His substance was seven thousand sheep, three thousand camels, five hundred yoke of oxen, five hundred asses, and a very great household. This man was the greatest of all the men of the east.

There came a day when the angels presented themselves before Jehovah, and Satan, the Evil One, came also among them. Jehovah spoke to Satan, saying, "Whence comest thou?"' and Satan answered, "From going to and fro upon the earth, from walking up and down upon it and observing people."

"Hast thou considered my servant, Job," Jehovah asked Satan, "that there is none like him on the earth, a perfect and an upright man, one that is god-fearing and shuns evil?" Satan answered, "It is easy for him to be good. Thou hast blessed the work of his hands and his wealth has increased, but put forth thine hand and take away what he has and he will curse thee to thy face."

Jehovah replied, "Behold, all that he has is in thy power, only upon himself put not thine hand." So Satan went forth from Jehovah's presence.

There came a day when Job's sons and daughters were eating food and drinking wine in their eldest brother's house and a messenger came to Job, saying, "Thy oxen were ploughing and the asses were feeding beside them when robbers fell upon them and took them away. Furthermore, the robbers have slain thy servants with the edge of the sword. I alone have escaped to tell thee." While he was speaking there came also another who cried out: "Fire has fallen from heaven and has burned up thy sheep and servants. I alone have escaped to tell thee." Then came another with the words: "The Chaldeans have fallen upon thy camels and have carried them away and have slain thy servants. I alone have escaped to tell thee." At that moment there came yet another, crying: "Thy sons and thy daughters were eating and drinking in their eldest brother's house when there came a great wind from the wilderness and struck the four corners of the house and it fell. I alone have escaped to tell thee."

Then Job arose, tore his clothes in grief but knelt on the ground, saying, "Jehovah gave and Jehovah has taken away. Blessed be the name of Jehovah." Again there was a day when the angels and Satan presented themselves before Jehovah and Jehovah asked Satan, "Hast thou now considered my servant Job?" Satan replied, "A man will give what he owns for his life. Put forth thine hand now and touch his bone and his flesh, and he will curse thee to thy face." "Behold," said Jehovah, "he is in thine hand, but take not his life."

So Satan went forth from Jehovah's presence and struck Job with sore boils from the sole of his foot to the crown of his head. Then his wife taunted him: "Dost thou still keep thy faith? Deny the heavenly powers and die." But he answered, "Thou speakest as one of the foolish women speaks. What? Shall we receive good at the hand of heaven and shall we not accept evil?"

Now when Job's three friends heard of all the misfortune that was come upon him, they came to mourn with him and to comfort him; but when they saw him, they scarcely knew him. They saw his grief was very great so they sat down with him but spoke not a word to him.

After a while Job opened his mouth and began to complain about the great measure of his suffering but his friends reproached him saying, "Suffering comes to those who have sinned or who forget the heavenly powers. Job is reaping the fruits of his wickedness." But Job was sure of his innocence and said to them, "Teach me wherein I have sinned and I will hold my tongue. Cause me to understand wherein I have erred."

Howbeit, his friends had no answer and accused him of lying, saying, "Thou speakest falsehoods," and Job replied, "It is you who speak words that are false. I suffer, and the wicked prosper; yet gods exist and the world is full of wisdom. There is reason for my suffering and I seek to understand it."

So these three men ceased to speak with Job because he was righteous in his own eyes. Then a fourth friend, Elihu, who had been listening, opened his mouth to speak. He was angry with Job because he justified himself, and angry with the other three because they condemned Job without cause. He said that no man should accuse the gods, that Job was lacking in knowledge and should strive to learn.

There came a whirlwind, and out of the whirlwind the voice of Jehovah, saying, "Who can judge without knowledge. Be strong, Job, and answer my questioning. Where wast thou when the Elohim laid the foundations of the earth? Who made the morning stars sing? Who closed the door of the sea so that there would be earth and water? Who causes the light and the darkness? Why were you born? Who causes the rain and who brings forth the flowers?"

Job was silent but said in his heart, "Forgive me, Lord, I am but as an ignorant child."

Then Jehovah spoke to him again out of the whirlwind, saying, "Be strong now and I will instruct thee. Behold the monster, Behemoth, whose bones are like iron, whose sinews are like stone. His teeth are terrible; his scales are his pride. Behold also Leviathan. Out of his mouth go burning lamps and sparks of fire. Upon earth there is not his like. He is king over all the children of pride."

Job saw these creatures, bowed to Jehovah and humbled himself, saying, "O Lord, I have spoken without understanding. Thou hast opened my eyes to see evil. My questioning will now be wiser."

Then Jehovah comforted Job, healed him, and gave him twice as much as he had before. So the latter end of Job's life was more blessed than the beginning, and he died, being old and full of days.

THE ISRAELITES IN EGYPT

Joseph and his brethren

JOSEPH'S DREAMS

Jacob had twelve sons and he loved Joseph more than the others because he was a child of his old age. He made him a coat of many colours but when his brothers saw that their father loved him more than he loved them, they hated Joseph and could not speak peaceably to him.

Now Joseph dreamed a dream and told it to his brothers. He said to them, "Hear, I pray you, about this dream that I have dreamed; behold, we were binding sheaves in the field and lo, my sheaf arose and stood upright and your sheaves bowed to my sheaf." Then his brothers were angry and answered, "Shalt thou indeed reign over us?" and they hated him all the more.

Another time Joseph dreamed yet another dream and told it to his brothers, saying, "I have dreamed another dream: the sun, the moon and the eleven stars bowed down before me." Then his father rebuked him with the words, "Shall I, thy mother, and thy brethren, bow down before thee?" but in his heart he remembered what Joseph had said.

In those days it was the custom of Joseph's brothers to take their father's flocks to feed in the field and, one day, Jacob told Joseph to go into the field to see if all was well with his brothers and to bring back news of them.

So Joseph bade farewell to his father and departed to seek his brothers.

From afar off they saw him coming and they conspired against him to slay him, saying to one another, "Behold this dreamer. Let us slay him and cast him into some pit and say that an evil beast has devoured him. We shall see what will become of his dreams." But Reuben set himself against this deed and said, "Let us not kill him, for he is our brother, but let us cast him into some pit and shed no blood," for Reuben thought to safeguard him and to return him again to his father.

JOSEPH IS SOLD INTO SLAVERY

Now when Joseph came into the presence of his brothers to do as his father had commanded, they stripped him of his coat of many colours, took him and cast him into a pit. Then they sat down to eat. Lifting up their eyes they saw a company of Ishmaelite merchants with their camels, bearing spices and myrrh down to Egypt and Judah said, "What profit is it to us to slay our brother? Let us sell him to the Ishmaelites and not stain our hands with his blood." So they lifted Joseph up out of the pit and sold him for twenty pieces of silver. It happened that Reuben had gone a little way off and when he returned to find Joseph no longer in the pit, he was sore perplexed.

Then the other brothers took Joseph's coat, dipped it into the blood of a kid and brought it to their father, saying, "This have we found. Is it thy son's coat?"

Jacob looked, knew it, tore his clothes in anguish and cried: "It is my son's coat. An evil beast has devoured him. Joseph is without doubt rent in pieces," and he mourned for his son and would not be comforted. Thus while his father wept for him, the merchants took Joseph to Egypt and there sold him to Potiphar, an officer of Pharaoh's, and captain of the guard.

IN POTIPHAR'S HOUSE

Now Joseph was a goodly person and Jehovah was with him. Potiphar perceived that Joseph was favored by Jehovah and he made him overseer over his house. All that Potiphar had he put in Joseph's hand. Jehovah also blessed Potiphar's house for Joseph's sake.

When Joseph was well established in the house of Potiphar, there came to him his master's wife to tempt him to do evil, but Joseph refused. One day when Joseph was alone in the house with his master's wife, she seized his garment to tempt him, but he fled, leaving his garment in her hands.

As soon as Potiphar returned to his house, she told him that Joseph had assailed her and he, believing her, became very angry. Thus it came about that Potiphar had Joseph put in prison, but Jehovah protected him and Joseph found favour with the keeper of the prison.

IN PRISON

Such esteem did Joseph find in the sight of the keeper of the prison that this same keeper committed to his hand all the prisoners and he looked not to anything that was in Joseph's care. Whatever Joseph did, Jehovah made it to prosper.

Now it happened that the chief butler of the king of Egypt and his baker had offended their master, the king of Egypt, and he put them into the prison with Joseph.

One night, they dreamed a dream, both of them, and in the morning they were sad of countenance. They spoke to Joseph, saying, "We have both dreamed dreams and there is no one to interpret them," but Joseph answered, "Are not interpretations to be sought from the powers in heaven? Tell me your dreams, I pray you, and I will help you."

First the chief butler told his dream. "In my dream," he said, "there was a vine before me with three branches. It was as though it budded and the clusters thereof brought forth ripe grapes. Pharaoh's cup was in my hand. I took the grapes, pressed them into the cup and gave it into Pharaoh's hand."

"This," said Joseph, "is the interpretation of thy dream: the three branches are three days; within three days shall Pharaoh restore thee to thy place. Remember me when thou art restored and make mention of me to Pharaoh, for I have done nothing for which I should be put into this prison."

When the chief baker saw that the interpretation was good, he said to Joseph, "In my dream I had three white baskets on my head. In the uppermost basket there was all manner of bakemeats for Pharaoh but the birds did eat them out of the basket on my head."

"This," said Joseph, "is the interpretation of thy dream: the three baskets are three days; within three days shall Pharaoh hang thee on a tree and the birds shall eat thy flesh from off thee."

On the third day after this, which was his birthday, Pharaoh made a great feast for his servants. He restored the butler to his former place that he might deliver again the cup into Pharaoh's hand, but he hanged the chief baker, as Joseph had foretold. Yet the chief butler did not remember Joseph but forgot him.

JOSEPH BECOMES GOVERNOR OF EGYPT

Two years after these things Pharaoh also dreamed a dream: there came up out of the river seven fat kine which fed in a meadow. After them came seven lean kine and the lean kine ate up the seven fat kine. So Pharaoh awoke.

A second time Pharaoh dreamed a dream: seven full ears of corn came up on one stalk. After them came seven thin ears and the seven thin ears devoured the seven full ears. So Pharaoh awoke and his spirit was troubled. He called for all the wise men in Egypt but none could interpret these dreams.

Then the chief butler remembered Joseph and spoke to Pharaoh, saying, "When Pharaoh was angry with his chief butler and with his chief baker and put them in prison, there was in that place with us a young man, a Hebrew, who interpreted our dreams and, as he interpreted to us, so it was."

When Pharaoh heard this, he sent his servants to bring Joseph forthwith out of prison and Pharaoh spoke to Joseph thus: "I have dreamed two dreams and there is no one that can tell me the interpretation thereof. I have heard it said that thou canst understand a dream and interpret it."

"Not by myself," answered Joseph, "but the Elohim will speak through me to give answer to Pharaoh."

So Pharaoh told Joseph his two dreams and Joseph declared: "The two dreams are one. The Elohim have shown Pharaoh what is to come. The seven fat kine are seven years; the seven full ears are seven years; there shall come seven years of great plenty throughout all the land of Egypt. The seven lean kine and the seven thin ears are seven years; after the years of plenty there shall come seven years of famine. All the plenty shall be forgotten and the famine following shall be grievous.

"Now, therefore, let Pharaoh look out a man, discreet and wise, and set him over the land of Egypt. Let Pharaoh do this and let him appoint officers over the land. Let them gather all the food of those good years and lay corn up under the hand of Pharaoh. That food shall be in store in the land against the years of famine."

This thing was good in the eyes of Pharaoh and he appointed Joseph to be overseer, saying, "Forasmuch as the powers of heaven have shown all this to thee, there is none so discreet and wise as thou art; thou shalt be ruler over my house and according to thy word shall all my people be ruled; only in the throne will I be greater than thou."

Pharaoh took off his ring from his hand and put it on Joseph's hand, arrayed him in vestures of fine linen, put a gold chain about his neck, made him to ride in the second chariot which he had, gave him to wife the daughter of Potipherah, priest of On, and made him ruler over all the land of Egypt.

Joseph was thirty years old when he became governor of Egypt. He gathered up the food in the cities. He gathered corn as the sand of the sea, very much, until he left numbering, for it was without number.

THE FAMINE

When the seven years of plenteousness were ended, there came the seven years of dearth. The famine was in all lands except in the land of Egypt where there was food. People of all countries came into Egypt to buy corn.

In the land of Canaan there was also famine. Therefore Jacob said to his sons, "Behold, I have heard that there is corn in Egypt;

get you down thither and buy for us that we may live and not die. Let my youngest son, Benjamin, stay with me lest mischief befall him. Since Joseph is gone, he is the only son remaining to me of my wife, Rachel."

JOSEPH'S BRETHREN COME TO EGYPT

So ten sons of Jacob went into Egypt to buy corn. They came before Joseph and bowed themselves before him, not knowing that he was their brother; but Joseph knew his brethren instantly and spoke roughly to them, asking them whence they came and what they desired. They told him that they were come from Canaan to buy food.

Joseph remembered the dreams which he had dreamed of them and said, "You are spies. You have come to spy out the land."

He questioned them further concerning their father and kindred and they answered, "Sire, we come to buy food. We are all one man's sons; we are true men; thy supplicants are no spies. Thy supplicants were twelve brothers; the youngest is this day with our father and one no longer lives."

Then Joseph answered, "You shall be proved. Send one of you and let him fetch your brother that your words may be proved whether there is any truth in you. In the meanwhile the rest will be kept in prison."

Then the brothers spoke among themselves that distress had come upon them because of their guilt concerning their brother, Joseph. They did not know that Joseph understood, for he had spoken to them through an interpreter.

On the third day after their coming, Joseph said, "Let it be thus: if you be true men, one of you shall remain as surety; the others go, carry corn for the famine of your houses but bring your youngest brother to me that your words may be verified."

Joseph took Simeon as a surety; then he commanded that their sacks be filled with corn and that every man's money be restored into his sack and that the men be given provision for the journey.

ON THE RETURN TO CANAAN

As the brothers rested on the way home, one of them opened his sack to give his ass provender and espied his money. When he told his brethren, they were all afraid.

At their homecoming Jacob rejoiced until they told him all that had befallen them and that the governor of Egypt had demanded that Benjamin be taken there. They emptied their sacks and behold, every man's money was in the mouth of his sack. Jacob was grieved and said, "Joseph and Simeon have been taken and now you will take Benjamin from me. He shall not go down. If mischief befall him on the way, then shall my grey hairs be brought with sorrow to the grave."

There was no ending to the famine. The food which the brothers had brought from Egypt was consumed and Jacob was constrained to say to his sons, "Go now again into the land of Egypt and buy us food that we may live." But Judah said to his father, "The man did protest to us, saying, 'You shall not see my face again unless your brother be with you.' If thou wilt not send our brother with us, we will not go down." Jacob asked why they had told the man about their younger brother and they answered, "The man asked concerning ourselves, our kindred, our father and our other brethren. Could we know what he would say?"

Then Judah spoke: "Send the lad with us and we will arise and go. I will be surety for him; if I bring him not back to thee, then let me bear the blame forever."

"If it must be so," replied Jacob, "then take the man a present; take also double money to pay back the money that was in the sacks; peradventure it was an oversight; take also your brother and may Jehovah Elohim preserve you before the man that he may send away your other brother and Benjamin."

THE SECOND VISIT TO EGYPT

So they took a present—double money—and Benjamin and went down to Egypt and stood once more before Joseph who said to his chief servant, "Bring these men to my house for they shall dine with me at noon."

At this the brothers were afraid but the steward said there was nothing of which they should be fearful and he brought Simeon to them.

When Joseph came home, they gave him their present and bowed themselves to the earth before him. He asked them of their welfare, whether their old father were yet alive and in good health, and if the boy be Benjamin, the youngest brother of whom they had spoken. Looking at Benjamin, Joseph's heart was moved that he made haste and sought a place to weep. When he could restrain himself, he came again and commanded that the meal be set before his guests.

Now Joseph desired to know of a certainty that his brothers no longer harboured unclean thoughts and that they were become true men and worthy. Therefore did he command the steward of his house to fill their sacks, to put the money back into the sacks, and to put his drinking cup into the sack of the youngest.

As soon as morning was light, the brothers departed. When they had gone but a little way, Joseph commanded his steward to follow them, overtake them and say, "Wherefore have you rewarded evil for good? Where is the cup from which my master drinks and divines? Who has taken it?"

They answered, "Wherefore says thy master these words? We are beholden to him and would not think of such a thing. The money which we found in our sacks before we brought again. How then should we steal silver and gold out of thy master's house? With whomsoever of thy supplicants it be found, let him die, and we also will be thy master's bondmen."

Then every man speedily took down his sack and opened it. The steward searched and the cup was found in Benjamin's sack.

Sore distressed, they returned to the city and came before Joseph who asked: "What deed is this that you have done? Do you not know that such a man as I can divine?"

Judah replied, "We know not what to say. We are in thy hand, both we and he also with whom the cup was found,"and Joseph answered, "The man in whose sack the cup was found shall be my servant; the others shall return in peace to their father."

Then Judah spoke again: "My Lord Governor, let not thine anger burn against thy supplicant. The lord governor asked concerning our father and brother and we told him of an old man and a child of his old age, a little one, and a brother who is no more. These two were sons of the same mother, who is dead, and our father loves the little one exceedingly and was loath to let him journey with us; but the lord governor said that without him we should not see his face. We therefore prevailed upon our father that the youngest come with us. Thy supplicant, even I, became surety for the lad. Now therefore, I pray thee, let me abide as bondman instead of the lad. Let the lad go with his brothers lest our father's grey hairs be brought with sorrow to the grave."

JOSEPH MAKES HIMSELF KNOWN TO HIS BRETHREN

Joseph could not refrain himself longer. He wept aloud and made himself known to his brethren, but his brethren were troubled at his presence. Then he spoke: "I am Joseph, your brother, whom you sold into Egypt. Come near to me. Be not grieved nor angry with yourselves for heavenly powers sent me before you to preserve life and to preserve you a posterity on the earth. It was not you that sent me hither but the Elohim. They have made me lord of all Pharaoh's house and ruler throughout all the land of Egypt. Haste ye, go to my father. Tell him that I have become governor of all Egypt. Say to him: come down and dwell in the land of Goshen, in Egypt, with thy children, thy children's children, flocks, herds and all that thou hast. There will I nourish thee, for there are yet five years of famine. Tell my father of all my glory in Egypt. Hasten and bring him hither."

Then Joseph embraced his brother, Benjamin, kissed his other brothers and talked with them.

Tidings of the coming of Joseph's brethren were brought to the court of Pharaoh. It pleased him well and he said to Joseph, "Tell your brethren to load their beasts, go to the land of Canaan, take wagons out of the land of Egypt for their little ones and their wives, bring your father, and tell them the good of all the land of Egypt is yours and theirs."

So Joseph sent his brethren back to Canaan and to Jacob with Pharaoh's message; and when they told Jacob all the words of Joseph and Pharaoh, his heart fainted, for he believed them not; but when he saw the wagons, his spirit revived and he said, "It is enough. Joseph, my son, is yet alive. I will go and see him before I die."

JACOB AND HIS FAMILY COME TO EGYPT

So Jacob gathered together all that he had, departed from Canaan and came to Beersheba. Here the Elohim appeared to him in a vision of the night and with one voice, said, "Jacob, we are the God of thy fathers; fear not to go down into Egypt. We will make of thee a great nation. We will go down with thee and we will surely bring thee up again."

Now Joseph had made ready his chariot to go forth to meet his father and when he saw him, he wept and embraced him. Jacob was content and said, "Now can I die in peace since I have seen thy face again."

Joseph brought Jacob his father to Pharaoh who bid him welcome and asked, "How old art thou?" and Jacob answered, "The years of my pilgrimage are a hundred and thirty years," and he blessed Pharaoh and went from his presence.

The sons of Jacob, who had been keepers of sheep, became keepers of cattle to Pharaoh, and Jacob himself lived in the land of Egypt for seventeen years. The time drew near for him to die. He called his sons to him and said, "I am about to die. Bury me, I pray you, with my fathers and kindred in the field at Hebron." Saying this, he blessed his sons and gave up the ghost.

When the days of mourning were passed, Joseph, with his brothers, all his household, and all the elders of the land of Egypt went to Canaan and buried the body of Jacob in Hebron, in the field which Abraham had bought.

After the death of Jacob, Joseph's brethren were troubled lest their brother should seek to requite them for the evil they had done to him but he, knowing their thoughts, spoke kindly to them, saying, "Fear not; you thought evil against me but the heavenly powers meant it for good, to save many people. I will nourish you and your little ones and comfort you."

So the children of Israel settled in Egypt and Joseph lived a hundred and ten years. When his time came to die, he called his brethren and said, "Elohim will surely visit you and bring you out of this land to the land promised to Abraham, to Isaac, and to Jacob. Carry my bones with you when you go from hence."

So Joseph died and was embalmed and put in a coffin in Egypt.

FROM EGYPT TO THE PROMISED LAND

Moses and his mission. Joshua

THE ISRAELITES ARE ENSLAVED

During their sojourn in Egypt the children of Israel increased abundantly, multiplied and grew exceeding mighty; and the land was filled with them.

Time passed and there arose a new king over Egypt who knew not Joseph. He said to his people, "Behold the people of the children of Israel are more and mightier than we. Let us deal wisely with them lest they multiply and perchance join our enemies and fight against us." Therefore he set hard taskmasters over them to afflict them with burdens, to make them build cities, and to do all manner of service in the field; but the more the taskmasters afflicted them, the more they multiplied and grew.

Then Pharaoh commanded that all male children born to the Israelites be thrown into the river.

THE BIRTH OF MOSES
PHARAOH'S DAUGHTER ADOPTS HIM

Now there was a woman of the house of Levi who found means to escape the command of Pharaoh. She bore a son, a goodly child, and hid him three months. When she could no longer hide him, she made an ark of bulrushes, daubed it with slime and with pitch, put the child therein, and laid it in the reeds by the river's brink. His sister stood afar off to see what would become of him.

In a little while the daughter of Pharaoh came down to bathe in the river, and when she saw the ark among the reeds, she sent her maid to fetch it. She opened it and saw the child, who wept. She had pity on it and said, "This is one of the Hebrews' children." Then the sister of the child came to her and asked, "Shall I go and call to thee a nurse of the Hebrew women that she may nurse the child for thee?"

Pharaoh's daughter agreed. The maid went away and called the child's mother. To her, Pharoah's daughter said, "Take this child and nurse it for me and I will give thee wages." Thus the woman nursed her own child and he grew and he was made Pharaoh's daughter's adopted son. She called his name Moses, and said, "Because I drew him out of the water." As Moses grew up, he learned all the wisdom of the Egyptians.

MOSES SLAYS AN EGYPTIAN AND FLEES

One day, when Moses was a grown man, he went out to his brethren and looked on their burdens and he saw an Egyptian striking a Hebrew. He looked this way and that. Seeing no one, he struck the Egyptian and killed him and hid his body in the sand.

The next day, he beheld two Hebrews fighting together. He asked the one that did the first wrong, "Why dost thou strike thy fellow?" and the man answered, "Who made thee a judge over us? Dost thou intend to kill me as thou hast killed the Egyptian?" Then Moses was afraid, fearing that this thing was known.

The tidings of this affray came to Pharaoh, who was angry and sought to slay Moses, but Moses fled. He went to the land of Midian and sat down by a well.

JETHRO, THE PRIEST OF MIDIAN

Now the priest of Midian had seven daughters and as Moses sat by the well, they came to draw water for their father's flock, but certain shepherds sought to drive them away. Then Moses stood up to protect the maidens and to help water their flock.

When they returned to their father, they told him all that had taken place and he said to his daughters, "Where is this man? Why have you left him? Call him that he may eat bread with us."

So Moses came to the house of Jethro, the priest of Midian, and he was made welcome and was content to dwell there. Jethro gave him his daughter, Zipporah, to wife, and he stayed for forty years.

In the meantime the children of Israel sighed by reason of their bondage. Their cry came up to the Elohim and the Elohim remembered their covenant with Abraham, Isaac and Jacob.

ON THE HOLY MOUNTAIN

Now Moses was keeper of his father-in-law's sheep and on a certain day, as he was leading the flock, he came to the holy mountain, even to Horeb.

There the Archangel Michael appeared unto him in a flame of fire out of the midst of the bush; but the bush was not consumed and Moses turned aside to see that great sight, why the bush was not burnt. He felt himself in the nearness of the Elohim and the Elohim called to him out of the midst of the bush: "Moses, Moses."

Moses answered, "Here I am."

Then the Elohim spoke as one, with one voice, saying, "Draw not nigh; put thy shoes from off thy feet for the place where thou standest is holy ground. We are the God of Abraham, of Isaac and of Jacob," but Moses hid his face for he was afraid to look upon gods.

Jehovah then spoke to Moses, "I have surely seen the affliction of my people who are in Egypt. I know their sorrows. I am come down to deliver them out of the hand of the Egyptians and to bring them to a land good and large, a land flowing with milk and honey. Therefore will I send thee to Pharaoh that thou mayest bring forth my people, the children of Israel, out of Egypt."

Moses turned to the Elohim and asked, "Who am I that I should go to Pharaoh and bring forth the children of Israel?"

"We shall be with thee," they replied.

Moses again spoke to the Elohim: "Behold, when I come to the people and shall say, 'The god of your fathers has sent me to you'; and they say, 'Who is this god? What is his name?' What shall I say?"

The Elohim answered, "Say, 'The I AM god has sent me to you.' Say, 'The god which enables man to say *I am* has sent me.' Say, "The Elohim and Jehovah Elohim have sent me.'"

Again Moses spoke: "They will not believe me."

Then Jehovah said to Moses, "Cast the rod which is in thine hand to the ground." Moses did as Jehovah bade; the rod became a serpent and he fled from it.

"Put forth thine hand," said Jehovah, "and take it by the tail," and it became a rod in his hand.

"Show this sign before the people," said Jehovah, "and they will believe thee. Now put thine hand into thy bosom."He did so and when he drew it forth again, behold, it was leprous as snow.

"Put thine hand into thy bosom once more," said Jehovah, and now when he plucked it out again, behold, it was as his other flesh.

"These are for signs to the people that I have spoken to thee." said Jehovah. "If they will not believe these two signs, take water out of the river and pour it onto the dry land. The water from the river will become blood."

Moses spoke again to Jehovah, saying, "O my Lord, I am not eloquent. I am slow of speech and of a slow tongue."

"Go," said Jehovah, "I will be with thy mouth and teach thee what thou shalt say. I know that Aaron, thy brother, can speak well. I will be with thy mouth and with his mouth and teach you what you shall do. Aaron shall be thy spokesman to the people. Take the rod in thine hand wherewith thou shalt do signs."

MOSES RETURNS TO EGYPT

After these things Moses returned to Jethro and asked that he might return to Egypt; and Jethro agreed, saying to him in friendly wise, "Go in peace." So Moses took his wife and his sons, his rod also, and returned to the land of Egypt.

Now Jehovah had told Aaron to go into the wilderness to meet Moses. They met in the holy mountain and went together to the elders of the children of Israel and did the signs in the sight of the people, and the people looked and believed.

Afterwards Moses and Aaron went to Pharaoh and spoke to him, saying, "Thus says Jehovah Elohim, the Lord God of Israel: Let my people go." But Pharaoh answered, "Who is this Lord that I should obey his voice to let Israel go? I know not this Jehovah, neither will I let Israel go. Moses, Aaron, get you to your burdens."

That same day Pharaoh commanded the taskmasters to lay heavier burdens on the children of Israel, saying, "You shall no more give the people straw to make bricks. Let them go and gather straw for themselves, but the number of bricks shall be as before. The children of Israel are idle, therefore they cry: let us go. Let more work be laid upon them."

So the taskmasters went forth and commanded the children of Israel to gather stubble and to make the same number of bricks as if they had straw; and the children of Israel saw that they were in evil case.

Therefore Moses returned to Jehovah and made complaint: "Lord, wherefore hast thou so evil entreated this people? Why is it that thou hast sent me? For since I came to Pharaoh to speak in thy name, he has done evil to this people; neither hast thou delivered thy people at all."

THE ELOHIM REVEAL THEIR NATURE

In answer to Moses, Jehovah said, "Thou shalt see what I shall do to Pharaoh. He must let my people go; but hearken now to the voice of the Elohim that thou mayest have understanding." Then the Elohim spoke to Moses, saying, "We and Jehovah are one, of one substance and of one nature. To Abraham, Isaac and Jacob we appeared as One, as God Almighty, but they knew not our name and nature. Be it known to thee that the name, Jehovah, means 'I am'."

JEHOVAH'S PROMISE

Jehovah spoke again: "I have remembered the covenant to bring the children of Israel out of their bondage in Egypt. Remind them that I, Jehovah Elohim, am their god and I will lead them into the promised land. Go now to Pharaoh. Tell him what I have said. Pharaoh will demand proof of my power. Then say thou to Aaron, ' Cast down thy rod before Pharaoh.' It will become a serpent."

Moses and Aaron did as Jehovah commanded. Pharaoh called his wise men and sorcerers. They also did in like manner and cast down every man his rod. The rods became serpents but Aaron's rod swallowed theirs up.

THE TEN PLAGUES

Jehovah spoke again to Moses: "Pharaoh's heart is hardened. Go to him in the morning; stand by the river's brink; take the rod in thy hand; say to Pharaoh: 'The Lord God of the Hebrews, Jehovah Elohim, has sent me to you. Thus says the Lord: Let my people go or all the waters of Egypt shall be turned to blood.'"

But Pharaoh's heart was hardened, and although the waters turned to blood, he would not let the people go.

Jehovah spoke again to Moses: "Go to Pharaoh. Say to him: 'Thus says the Lord: Let my people go. If thou refuse, I will strike all thy borders with frogs. They shall come into thy house, into thy bedchamber, into thy bed, into the houses of all thy people everywhere.'"

But Pharaoh took no heed. Aaron stretched out his hand and the frogs came up and covered the land.

Pharaoh called Moses and Aaron and said, "Entreat the Lord that he take away the frogs and I will let your people go." Moses and Aaron did so. Jehovah removed the frogs. Pharaoh saw that there was respite and refused to let the people go.

Jehovah spoke again to Moses: "Say to Aaron: 'Strike the dust of the land that it become lice.'" Aaron did so. All the dust of the land became lice and covered all the land of Egypt. Pharaoh called his wise men and sorcerers but they could not remove the lice. Still Pharaoh would not let the people go.

Jehovah spoke again to Moses: "Go to Pharaoh. Say to him: 'Thus says Jehovah: Let my people go or I will send swarms of flies upon thee, thy servants, thy people, into their houses, all over the ground.'"

But Pharaoh would not hear and the people were not set free. Then came the flies and filled the air and covered the ground. Pharaoh called Moses and Aaron and said, "Entreat the Lord that he take away the flies and I will let your people go." Moses and Aaron did so. Jehovah removed the flies. Pharaoh saw that there was respite and would not let the people go.

Jehovah spoke again to Moses: "Go to Pharaoh. Say to him: 'Thus says Jehovah: Let my people go or I will send a grievous murrain on thy cattle, horses, asses, camels, oxen and sheep.'"

Still Pharaoh would not let the people go; and the murrain visited the cattle, horses, asses, camels, oxen and sheep. Jehovah spoke again to Moses: "Go to Pharaoh. Sprinkle a handful of ashes toward heaven in front of him. The ashes shall become as small dust and bring forth boils and sores on the people of Egypt." Moses did so and all the people of Egypt were visited with boils and sores.

But Pharaoh was not moved and the people stayed.

Jehovah spoke again to Moses: "Go to Pharaoh. Say to him: 'Thus says Jehovah: Let my people go or I will spread pestilence over thee and thy people. I will send hail and fire from heaven.'"

Still Pharaoh would not let the people go. The pestilence came.

Pharaoh called Aaron and Moses to him and said to them, "I have sinned this time. Jehovah is righteous. I and my people are wicked. Entreat the Lord that there be no more mighty thunderings and hail and I will let the people go."

Moses spread abroad his hands, to Jehovah. The thunders and the hail ceased. Pharaoh saw that there was respite and kept the people there.

Jehovah spoke yet again to Moses: "Go to Pharaoh. Say to him: 'Thus says Jehovah: Let my people go or I will bring locusts into thy land. They shall consume all herb and tree and cover the face of the earth.'"

Still Pharaoh would not let the people go. The east wind blew and brought the locusts. They covered the face of the earth and ate every herb and all the fruit of the trees until there remained not any green thing in all the land of Egypt.

Pharaoh called Moses and Aaron and said, "Entreat the Lord that he take away the locusts and I will let the people go."

Moses entreated Jehovah and Jehovah sent a mighty strong west wind which took away the locusts and cast them into the Red Sea. Pharaoh saw that there was respite and the people stayed.

Jehovah spoke again to Moses: "Stretch out thine hand toward heaven that there may be darkness over the land of Egypt." Moses did so and darkness which could be felt spread over the land.

Pharaoh called Moses and said, "Go now with thy people but leave behind your flocks and your herds." Moses answered, "The flocks and herds are ours; they shall come with us."

Pharaoh was angry and he charged Moses: "Get thee from me. Let me see thy face no more. In that day thou seest my face thou shalt die."

Moses answered, "Thou hast spoken well. I will see thy face again no more."

Now all these wonders did Moses and Aaron do before Pharaoh to the Egyptians and the land of Egypt, but the children of Israel and the land of Goshen, where they lived, were not afflicted.

Jehovah spoke again to Moses: "I will bring one more plague upon Egypt. Afterwards, Pharaoh will let you go. About midnight all the first-born of the Egyptians shall die and there shall be a great cry throughout all the land of Egypt such as there was none before like it."

THE PASSOVER

Then to Moses and to Aaron Jehovah said, "Speak to all the congregation of Israel and say: In the tenth day of this month every household shall take a lamb, keep it until the fourteenth day, then slay it and smear the doorposts with its blood, roast the flesh and eat it in the night. I will pass through the land of Egypt this night and will strike all the first-born in the land; but where I see blood on the doorposts, these houses will I pass over. This day shall you keep as a memorial and as a festival forever. Say to the people: It is the festival of the Passover."

Moses, Aaron, and the people, obeyed and did as Jehovah had commanded them; and in the night there arose a great cry throughout Egypt, for there was not a house where there was not one dead.

THE ISRAELITES ARE RELEASED

Pharaoh rose up in the night, called for Moses and Aaron and said, "Rise up and get you forth from among my people. Take your flocks and your herds and be gone and bless me also."

The Egyptians urged the children of Israel to depart at once and they went forth in such haste that they had to take with them dough which was unleavened, neither had they prepared for themselves any victual. They were about six hundred thousand, not counting children; and the sojourning of the children of Israel in Egypt was four hundred and thirty years.

CROSSING THE RED SEA

The Israelites now came into the wilderness and Jehovah led them by day in a pillar of cloud and by night in a pillar of fire. Moses took the bones of Joseph with them as Joseph had desired.

After the children of Israel were gone forth from Egypt, it grieved Pharaoh that they were no longer there to serve him. Therefore he made ready his chariot to follow them and commanded his charioteers, his horsemen and his army, to pursue them and bring them back.

The Israelites were encamped by the sea when they espied the Egyptians coming near and they were sore afraid, but Moses said, "Fear not; stand still. See the salvation of Jehovah which he will show you today. The Egyptians who come near will be seen no more again for ever."

Jehovah spoke to Moses, saying, "Lift up thy rod; stretch out thine hand over the sea and divide it, for the children of Israel shall go on dry land through the midst of the sea."

Moses stretched out his hand over the sea. Jehovah caused a strong east wind and the waters divided. The children of Israel went into the midst of the sea upon dry ground; the waters formed a wall on their right hand and on their left.

The Archangel Michael, who went in front of the host of Israel, removed and went behind it. He came between the host of Israel and the host of the Egyptians. To these he was a cloud and a darkness, but to the Israelites, a light. The Egyptians pursued and went in after them into the midst of the sea.

Jehovah said to Moses, "Stretch out thine hand over the sea." He did so and the waters returned behind them and covered the chariots, the horsemen, and all the host of Pharaoh, but the children of Israel walked on dry land in the midst of the sea and came safely to the far shore.

BITTER WATERS ARE MADE SWEET

After three days journeying through the wilderness the people were thirsty. They found water but it was bitter and they could not drink it, and they murmured against Moses, saying, "What shall we drink?" Moses cried to Jehovah and Jehovah told him to cast a certain tree into the waters. He did as commanded and behold, the waters were made sweet that all could satisfy their thirst.

In the second month of their journeying the Israelites again murmured against Moses: "We are hungry. Would that we had stayed in Egypt. There we sat by the flesh-pots and did eat bread to the full. Now thou hast brought us to this wilderness to die of hunger."

MANNA FROM HEAVEN

Then Jehovah spoke to Moses: "I have heard the murmurings of the children of Israel. Speak to them. Say: 'At even you shall eat flesh and in the morning you shall be filled with bread.' You shall know that I am Jehovah Elohim, the Lord your God."

At even quails came up and covered the camp so that they could easily be caught. In the morning the dew lay round about but when the dew was gone, behold, on the face of the wilderness lay many small round things. The people looked and said *manna*, which means 'What is it?' Moses told them that it was bread which Jehovah had sent them to eat and that it must be collected and ground fresh daily except on the sixth day when enough could be gathered to tide over the Sabbath.

Until they came to the borders of Canaan, after forty years in the wilderness, this was the food of the children of Israel.

WATER FROM THE ROCK

The congregation of the people journeyed further into the desert and there was again no water for them to drink. They murmured again against Moses, saying, "In Egypt we had water. Now thou has brought us to this wilderness to die of thirst."

Again Jehovah spoke to Moses: "Go on before thy people to the rock in Horeb. Take thy rod, strike the rock, and water shall come out of it." Moses did so and the people had water.

JETHRO'S ADVICE

When Jethro, the priest of Midian, Moses' father-in-law, heard that Jehovah had brought the children of Israel out of Egypt, he came to meet Moses in the wilderness and they met at the holy mountain.

Moses told his father-in-law of the deliverance of his people and Jethro rejoiced. Together they made celebration.

The next day Moses sat to judge his people's disputes, but when Jethro observed how he was occupied from morning to evening, he said, "The thing that thou doest is not good. Thou wilt surely wear away. This thing is too heavy for thee. Hearken now to my voice. I will give thee counsel. Be thou for the people spokesman with the heavenly powers and be interpreter between them and the people. Teach thy people ordinances and laws and the work that they must do, but appoint able, godfearing men, men of truth, to judge people in thy place. Every great matter shall be brought to thee but every small matter shall be judged by those whom thou has appointed."

The counsel that his father-in-law gave to Moses seemed good to him and he did all that he had said.

MOSES RECEIVES THE TEN COMMANDMENTS

The children of Israel were now encamped near the holy mountain of Sinai. Moses went alone up into the mount and Jehovah appeared to him and said, "Go to the people. Sanctify them today and tomorrow. Let them wash their clothes and be ready for the third day. On that day Jehovah will come down on Mount Sinai in the sight of all the people. Set bounds for the people that they come not up into the mountain or touch the borders of it for fear of death. When the trumpet sounds long, they shall come to the foot of the mount."

On the third day, there were thunderings and lightnings and a thick cloud upon the mountain. The voice of the trumpet spoke exceeding loud that all the people trembled. Jehovah descended in smoke and fire and the mountain quaked greatly. From the top of the mountain Jehovah called to Moses to tell the people not to come too close lest they perish. Then speaking on behalf of the Elohim, he proclaimed:

"I am the Lord thy God, Jehovah Elohim, which brought thee out of the land of Egypt, out of the house of bondage.

Thou shalt have no other gods before me.

Thou shalt not make for thyself any graven image, or any likeness of anything that is in heaven above, or in the earth beneath or in the water under the earth. Thou shalt not bow down to it nor worship it.

Thou shalt not take the name of the Lord thy God in vain.

Remember the Sabbath day, to keep it holy. Six days shalt thou labour and do all thy work but the seventh day is the Sabbath of the Lord thy God.

Honour thy father and thy mother.

Thou shalt not kill.

Thou shalt not commit adultery.

Thou shalt not steal.

Thou shalt not bear false witness against thy neighbour.

Thou shalt not covet thy neighbour's house, nor thy neighbour's wife, nor his manservant, nor his maidservant, nor his ox, nor his ass, nor anything that is thy neighbour's."

The people saw the thunderings and the lightnings, heard the voice of the trumpet, saw the mountain smoking, removed themselves, and stood afar off; but Moses drew near to the thick darkness on the mountain.

There Jehovah gave him instruction in how the people should live and behave; and Moses came down from the mountain, told the words of Jehovah to the people and wrote them down.

The glory of Jehovah and the covering cloud rested on Mount Sinai for six days and the sight of the glory of Jehovah was like devouring fire on the top on the mount in the eyes of the children of Israel. On the seventh day Jehovah again called Moses to come to him, and Moses went up the mount into the midst of the cloud and stayed there for forty days and forty nights.

When Jehovah had made an end of communing with him, he gave him two tablets of testimony, of stone, written by his own divine hand.

THE GOLDEN CALF

When the people saw that Moses delayed to come down from the mountain, they said to Aaron, "Up, make us gods which shall go before us. As for this Moses, we know not what has become of him."

Aaron demanded of them their golden earrings and fashioned them into a molten calf which they began to worship. Then

Moses came down from the mount with the two tablets of testimony in his hand. As soon as he saw the golden calf and the dancing, he was exceeding angry. He cast the tablets out of his hand and broke them. He took the calf, burnt it in the fire, ground it to powder, strewed it upon water, and made the children of Israel drink of it.

He said to the people, "You have sinned a great sin yet are still the chosen people. I will go to Jehovah; peradventure I shall make atonement for your sin."

Moses spoke with Jehovah and Jehovah answered, "Whosoever has sinned against me, him will I blot out of my book; but go, lead the people to the place of which I have spoken to thee. My angel shall go before thee. Hew thee two tablets of stone like the first and I will write upon these tablets the words which were in the first. Come in the morning to Mount Sinai and present thyself to me at the top. Let no man come with thee."

THE COVENANT RENEWED

So Moses rose up early and did as commanded. Jehovah told him again what was required of the people, and the words of the covenant, the ten commandments, were written anew on the tablets. Moses wrote the words down as Jehovah dictated them. When Moses came down from the mount, Aaron and all the children of Israel saw that the skin of his face shone and they were afraid to come near him. He therefore spoke to them with a veil before his face.

THE TABERNACLE IS BUILT

The children of Israel had now journeyed for several months through the wilderness and they had no abiding place in which to worship, but while Moses was in the mount, Jehovah had commanded him that a sanctuary, a tabernacle, be built. This was to serve as a passing house of worship which could accompany the people of their journeyings. Jehovah also commanded that a chest be made, an ark, to hold the writings of the law, and that this should rest within the tabernacle. Priests should be appointed to serve therein.

Jehovah named two cunning workmen, Bezaleel and Aholiab, to oversee the work.

According to the words of Jehovah, brought down by Moses, the children of Israel applied themselves to the task of building the tabernacle. They took boards of fine wood and overlaid them with gold. They made fine woven curtains, white, blue, purple and scarlet, and coverings of rams' skins, dyed red. They made all measurements in strict accordance with the word of Jehovah and they brought jewels, gold, silver, fine cloth for decorations, oil for the light, and spices for sweet incense.

Bezaleel made the ark of acacia wood, overlaid the wood with fine gold within and without and set a crown of gold upon it. He put four rings of gold in the four corners and made staves overlaid with gold to put through the rings that the ark might be carried on them.

He also made a mercy seat of pure gold and figures of two Cherubim, beaten out of one piece of gold, on the two ends thereof. The Cherubim spread out their wings on high over the mercy seat with their faces turned to one another.

He made a table covered with gold and a golden candlestick to set thereon; also two altars of acacia wood, one covered with gold and one with brass.

In the ark Moses placed the two tablets which he had received from Jehovah on the mountain.

Jehovah commanded Moses that Aaron and his sons become priests. Fine raiment and apparel, to serve as holy garments, were made for them.

When the work was finished, a cloud covered the tabernacle and it was filled with Jehovah's glory.

Henceforth when the cloud was lifted up from off the tabernacle, the children of Israel journeyed. In the places where the cloud rested, the people also rested. Whether it was by day or by night that the cloud was lifted up, they journeyed; whether it were two days, or a month, or a year that the cloud tarried upon the tabernacle, they journeyed not.

The children of Israel became weary again of their journey through the wilderness and again they murmured against Moses. Jehovah was angered and sent quails from the sea; but before they could be eaten, he sent a plague and many men perished.

SCOUTS ARE SENT TO SPY OUT THE LAND

Moses now sent twelve men to spy out the land of Canaan; of each tribe he sent one man. Among them were Joshua and Caleb.

The scouts returned after forty days bringing with them a huge bunch of grapes, pomegranates and figs, and said, "We came to the land whither we were sent and surely it flows with milk and honey. Nevertheless, the people be strong that dwell in that land; the cities are walled and very great."

Caleb said, "Let us go up at once and possess it, for we are well able to overcome it," but others brought an evil report of the land, saying, "We are not able to go up against this people. We saw men of great stature, giants, against whom we are like grasshoppers."

Then the children of Israel wept and cried, "Would that we had died in Egypt. Were it not better for us to return? Let us make a captain and go back."

Joshua and Caleb spoke up, saying that the land was indeed good and that Jehovah would stand by them, but the people grew all the more angry and spoke bitter words.

Jehovah heard and spoke to Moses and Aaron, saying, "How long shall I bear with this evil congregation who have not trust in me or believe me in spite of all the wonders that I have done before them? Lo, the children of Israel shall wander forty years in the wilderness and there die and their bodies be wasted; and, except the little ones, they shall not enter the promised land. Of the men who went to search the land, Joshua and Caleb shall enter it, the ten others even now shall die by the plague."

KORAH'S REBELLION

Others also of the children of Israel caused grief to Moses and Aaron. Korah, with two hundred and fifty of the princes of Israel, gathered themselves together against Moses and Aaron, and demanded to know why these two lifted themselves up above the rest of the congregation.

Moses answered them saying that every one of them should bring a censer with burning incense and meet him the next day before the tabernacle, when Jehovah would pass judgment. In the morning the two hundred and fifty princes stood at the door of the tabernacle with the congregation of the people around them, but Korah and two other rebels would not come.

Then Moses spoke to all the people, saying, "Separate yourselves from these three men and touch nothing of theirs. Hereby you shall know that Jehovah has sent me to do this work. If the earth open up and swallow the three, then you shall understand that they have provoked Jehovah. Stand aside also from the tabernacle."

As he made an end of speaking these words, the ground under Korah and his two companions burst asunder. The earth opened her mouth and swallowed them up. In the same moment fire blazed forth and consumed the two hundred and fifty men who had brought incense.

APPOINTMENT OF AARON

Now Jehovah was wearying of the people's complaints and said to Moses, "I will make an end of the murmurings of the children of Israel and will appoint one to be my special servant in the guidance of my people. Tell the leader of each tribe to write his name on a rod and to bring it to you. Put the rods together in the tabernacle. The rod of the one I have chosen to be high priest will blossom."

The rods were taken and put in the tabernacle. The next morning Moses brought out all the rods in the sight of the people and lo, Aaron's rod had brought forth buds and bloomed blossoms.

On their further journeyings the children of Israel came into the desert of Zin and they abode in Kadesh. Again there was no water and again the people gathered themselves together against Moses and Aaron, chiding them for bringing them out of the land of Egypt.

MOSES DOUBTS

Moses and Aaron prayed for help and the glory of Jehovah appeared unto them. Jehovah spoke to Moses and said, "Take thy rod, strike the rock and it shall give forth water for all the congregation and their beasts."

So Moses and Aaron gathered the people before the rock but in their hearts they doubted whether the power of Jehovah would bring forth the water. Moses lifted the rod and struck the rock. No water came forth. He struck it a second time and only on the second stroke did the water gush forth. Then Jehovah complained to Moses and Aaron, saying, "You have cast doubt on my power in the eyes of the people. You doubted, and therefore you shall not bring this congregation into the promised land."

AARON DIES

After their sojourn in Kadesh the children of Israel came to Mount Hor and the time was come for Aaron to die. In accordance with Jehovah's command, Moses, Aaron and Aaron's son, Eleazar, climbed to the top of the mount where Moses took off Aaron's vestments and put them on Eleazar. There, at the top of the mount, Aaron died and was mourned by the whole house of Israel.

THE BRAZEN SERPENT

To avoid the land of Edom, whose king was hostile to them, the Israelites journeyed from Mount Hor by way of the Red Sea. Again they felt grieved at their lot and complained. Jehovah answered by sending fiery serpents which bit the people and thereafter many died. Moses prayed to Jehovah and received counsel what he should do.

As Jehovah had instructed him, so did Moses make a serpent of brass, fastened by the head upon a pole; and it came to pass that if a serpent had bitten any man, when he beheld the serpent, he lived.

BALAAM AND HIS ASS

From the Red Sea the children of Israel came into the plains of Moab on this side of the River Jordan, by Jericho. The king of the Moabites, Balak, was sore afraid of the people of Israel because they were so many. He sent for Balaam, a sorcerer, to come and curse them, but heavenly beings appeared to Balaam to tell him that this people were blessed and that he should not go.

Unheeding, Balaam saddled his ass the next morning and rode out. As he journeyed, an angel stood in the way. The ass saw him and turned aside into a field. Balaam had not seen the angel and beat the ass to turn her back to the road. She made her way along a path with walls on either side of it, and again the angel stood before her. She turned aside and crushed Balaam's foot against the wall. A second time he beat her but now she came into a narrow passage where there was no room to turn and again the angel blocked the way. When the ass saw the angel this time, she fell down under Balaam and he beat her with a stick. Then the ass opened her mouth and asked why she was beaten. "Because thou mockest me," answered Balaam but at that moment Jehovah opened his eyes. He saw the angel, bowed his head and repented that he had beaten his beast. The angel told him to go on his way but to speak only the words that he, the angel, would tell him.

BALAAM PROPHESIES THE COMING OF THE MESSIAH

Balaam came to the king of Moab who had made all preparation for the cursing. Then Balaam opened his mouth and said:

How shall I curse those whom the powers of heaven have not cursed?

How shall I defy whom Jehovah has not defied?

Behold! I have received commandment to bless.

How goodly are thy tabernacles, O Israel!

There shall come a Star out of Jacob

And a sceptre shall rise out of Israel.

Blessed is he that blesses thee!

And cursed is he that curses thee!

Then Balak's anger was kindled against Balaam, but Balaam rose up and went back to his place.

MOSES DIES

The time came when Moses should leave the earth and another leader be appointed. Jehovah said to Moses, "Take thee Joshua, the son of Nun, a man in whom is the spirit, and lay thine hand upon him. Set him before Eleazar the priest and before all the congregation. He shall be made leader in their sight."

Moses did as the Lord commanded, laid his hands upon Joshua, and the children of Israel hearkened unto him. Moses then spoke to all the congregation. He set forth how they had suffered and struggled and what Jehovah had promised. He recited the laws and the commandments and enjoined the people to obey them. In mighty words he declared the greatness of the God of Israel and gave the people his blessing.

That selfsame day Jehovah spoke these words to Moses: "Get thee up into this mountain Abarim, to mount Nebo, and look upon the land of Canaan which I give to the children of Israel. Thou shalt see the land as I have promised thee but go thither thou mayest not."

So Moses went up into the mountain and he looked upon the land of Canaan. There on the mount he died, and he was buried in a valley in the land of Moab, but no man knows his sepulchre to this day.

Moses was a hundred and twenty years old when he died. His eye was not dim, nor his natural force abated. There arose no other prophet in Israel like Moses, whom Jehovah knew face to face, and the children of Israel wept for Moses thirty days.

JOSHUA BECOMES LEADER

After the death of Moses Jehovah spoke to Joshua, saying, "Moses, my servant, is dead; now therefore arise, go over this Jordan to the land which I give to the children of Israel. As I was with Moses, so I will be with thee. Be strong and of good courage. Observe the law, for then shall thy way be prosperous. The Lord thy God, Jehovah Elohim, is with thee."

SCOUTS ARE AGAIN SENT INTO CANAAN

Before entering the promised land, Joshua sent out two men to spy out the country. They lodged in Jericho with a woman called Rahab. Word of the spies was brought to the king and he sent soldiers to seek them out but the woman hid them. When the soldiers had gone, Rahab made known to them her belief in the god of the Israelites and her belief that the Israelites should come to dwell in Canaan. She told them that the inhabitants of the city were faint for fear and she asked for a token that would save her and her family when the city was taken. The men gave her a piece of scarlet cord to hang in her window. She then let them down by a rope to the outside of the city, for her house was built upon the city wall.

Thus the two men escaped and came to Joshua and they told him all that had befallen them and of the fear of those who dwelt in Jericho.

CROSSING THE JORDAN

Joshua then ordered the people to prepare to cross the River Jordan in the way Jehovah had commanded him; and the crossing was made in this wise: the priests carried the Ark of the Covenant before the people and, as their feet dipped in the water of the river, the waters which came down were cut off and the priests stood on firm ground in the midst of the river while the congregation passed over on dry ground. Joshua ordered that twelve stones be taken from the river bed and reared up on the further bank as a memorial. He also commanded that twelve stones be set in the river bed where the priests had stood. They are there to this day.

When all the people and the priests had reached the further shore, the waters returned to their usual place.

The Israelites then made celebration and ate cakes made of corn of the land of Canaan and the fruit thereof. The manna ceased to fall and the name of the place was called Gilgal.

THE ARCHANGEL MICHAEL APPEARS TO JOSHUA

As Joshua looked towards Jericho, he saw the figure of an angel before him with a drawn sword in his hand. The angel said to Joshua, "As captain of the host of Jehovah am I now come. The place where thou standest is holy ground." Then Joshua bowed down, for he knew it was the Archangel Michael.

JERICHO IS CAPTURED

Now Jericho was a walled city, carefully guarded. None went out and none came in. Jehovah gave word to Joshua how to take the city and according to his word, so was it done.

Seven priests, blowing trumpets of ram's horns, led a procession. After them came armed men, then the Ark of the Covenant, borne by priests; then more armed men. The company compassed the city daily for six days. On the seventh day they marched round the city seven times. At the seventh time the priests blew a great blast on their trumpets, the people shouted with a great shout, and the walls of the city fell down flat.

The Israelites had been enjoined not to plunder or to take spoil for themselves but one man took silver, gold and Babylonian things and buried them in his tent. Others also transgressed Jehovah's law but retribution came in this manner:

AI IS ATTACKED

After Jericho had fallen into their hands, the Israelites went up against Ai, but the men of Ai smote them that they fled. Then Joshua was grieved and complained to Jehovah, but Jehovah answered, "The people sinned in Jericho and did evil; therefore seek out the guilty ones that thy hosts may be purified." So Joshua made enquiry, found the guilty persons and punished them.

Then the hosts of Israel went up again to the city of Ai and captured it. Joshua built an altar there and made offerings to Jehovah and on the stones of the altar he wrote a copy of the law of Moses in the presence of all the people. Afterwards he read to them all the words of the law as Moses had written them.

CANAAN IS CONQUERED

Besides the Canaanites, there were also in that land other peoples with whom the Israelites had to contend—the Hittites, the Amorites, the Perizzites, the Jebusites and many others.

When the inhabitants of Gibeon heard what Joshua had done to Jericho, they were afraid for themselves and did work wilily. Their ambassadors put old rags on their asses, old garments and old shoes upon themselves, sour wine in their bottles, and stale bread in their packs. They came to Joshua and said, "We are from a far country and have heard of the fame of Jehovah Elohim, the Lord God of the Israelites; now therefore make a league with us. Our garments and our shoes are worn out by reason of our long journey." Joshua beheld them and made a league with them, promising that they would not be harmed.

Howbeit, after three days Joshua learned that they were neighbours and came not from far distant as they had said; yet because of his promise he spared them but, because of their deceit, he made them hewers of wood and drawers of water for the congregation of Israel.

Five neighbouring kings were angry when they heard that the Gibeonites had made a league with Joshua and they made war against them. Joshua, with his men of valor, went forth to do battle against these kings and their hosts. When he saw their mighty armies before him, he looked up to heaven and cried with a loud voice: "Spirit of the Sun, stand by us." Then were the armies of the five kings discomforted and fled before the hosts of Israel.

When, after much struggle, the whole of the land of Canaan was delivered into the hand of Joshua, he divided it among the twelve tribes according to the sons of Jacob, that each tribe had its own fitting portion.

Thus the Israelites possessed the land that had been promised to them and there was rest. Joshua grew old and stricken in age and he called for the elders of Israel. He reminded them of their great leaders, of the laws of their god, of their heritage, and of their charge. He took a great stone and set it up under an oak tree, saying, "Behold! this stone shall be a witness lest ye deny your god."

After these things, Joshua, the servant of Jehovah, died. He was one hundred and ten years old.

APPOINTMENT OF JUDGES

Guidance and encouragement

In Canaan there grew up generations who knew neither Moses, nor Joshua, nor the works of Jehovah which he had done for Israel. They forsook the god of their fathers and followed the gods of the people about them, serving Baal and Ashtaroth. Then the anger of Jehovah was kindled against them and he delivered them up to their enemies that they might repent of their wickedness.

But to guide the people back to the way of their fathers Jehovah also raised up 'judges,' not to judge the people but to lead and direct them. As often as they hearkened to their judge, so often were they freed from oppression but as often as they hearkened not, so often came they again into the hands of their enemies.

GIDEON IS CALLED

Among the judges appointed by Jehovah was one called Gideon, the youngest son of a poor man called Joash.

At that time the children of Israel had been delivered into the hands of their enemies and their food was scant. Gideon was threshing wheat secretly to hide it from the taskmasters when the Archangel Michael appeared to him and said, "Jehovah is with thee, thou mighty man of valour. Go in thy might and thou shalt save Israel."

Gideon answered, "O my Lord, if Jehovah be with us, why then is all this misfortune befallen us. Jehovah has forsaken us, delivered us into the hands of our enemies, and we starve. My family is poor. I am the least in my father's house. How shall I save Israel?"

The angel spoke again, saying, "Jehovah will be with thee," and he departed in a flash of fire.

Then Gideon heard Jehovah's voice which told him to cast down the altar of Baal. He took with him ten men and did so.

After this Gideon wished for a sign from heaven that he was chosen to lead Israel and he said to the Elohim, "If you will save Israel by my hand, behold, I will put a fleece of wool on the floor. If the dew be on the fleece only, and it shall be dry upon the earth beside, then shall I know that Israel shall be saved through me." When Gideon rose up in the morning to behold the fleece, lo, the dew was in it and the ground was dry.

He prayed again: "Let not the anger of the Elohim be against me but this night let it be dry upon the fleece and on the ground let there be dew," and in the morning it was so.

So Gideon gathered together the hosts of the Israelites to free themselves from their enemies but Jehovah said to him, "The number of men with thee is too many, lest they vaunt themselves against me and say: Our own hand has saved us. Proclaim therefore that whoever is afraid shall turn back." Gideon did as commanded and twenty-two thousand turned back. Ten thousand remained.

Again Jehovah spoke to Gideon: "The numbers are yet too many. Bring the men down to the water and I will test them for thee. Every man that takes water in his hand and then laps it as a dog laps, set him aside. Do likewise with those who kneel."

There were three hundred who took up water in their hands and lapped it and Jehovah said to Gideon, "These three hundred men shall win you deliverance."

GIDEON'S VICTORY

That same night Jehovah spoke again to Gideon: "Go with thy servant down to the host of the enemy, outside his camp, and thou shalt hear what they say."

Gideon and his servant went down to where the enemy host lay along the valley, like grasshoppers for multitude. Their camels were without number, like the sand by the sea. Gideon and his servant stood secretly outside the camp and heard the voice of a man who told a dream to his fellow. His words were: "I have dreamed a dream. A cake of barley tumbled into our midst, came to a tent and overturned it." His fellow answered, "This is nothing else save the sword of Gideon for into his hand will heaven deliver us."

When Gideon heard the telling of the dream and the interpretation thereof, he returned to the host of Israel. He divided the three hundred men into three companies, put a trumpet and a lamp in an empty pitcher in every man's hand and said, "Look on me when we go forth and do as I do. When we come to the outside of the camp and I blow with a trumpet, then blow you the trumpets and cry: 'The sword of Jehovah and of Gideon'" They came to the outside of the camp in the middle watch of the night. They blew their trumpets and broke the pitchers and held the lamps in their left hands and shouted: "The sword of Jehovah and of Gideon!"

When the hosts of the enemy heard the noise of the shouting and the breaking of the pitchers and saw the lamps, they were sore afraid and fled.

Thus were they subdued and they lifted up their heads no more; and after these things there was quietness in the land for forty years.

As for Gideon, he died in good old age; but no sooner was he dead than the children of Israel began again to do evil in the sight of Jehovah.

THE STRONG MAN, SAMSON

Because the Israelites again transgressed, Jehovah delivered them into the hand of the Philistines for forty years; but when the time was fulfilled, he sent new judges. One of the greatest of these was Samson.

There was, among the children of Israel, a man called Manoah, and as yet his wife had borne no children. Then one day the Archangel Michael appeared to her and said, "Behold, thou shalt bear a son; drink no wine and eat no unclean thing. The child shall be a Nazarite; the hair on his head shalt not be shorn. He will begin to deliver Israel out of the hand of the Philistines."

When the child was born, he was called Samson (Son of the Sun). Jehovah blessed him; the spirit of Jehovah moved him and he grew to be a man of mighty strength.

When he was grown to be a man, a certain woman of the Philistines pleased him well and he desired to take her to wife. She lived in a city a little way distant and as Samson went to visit her, a lion roared against him but he slew it with his bare hands and continued his journey. On returning, he turned aside to see the carcass of the lion and behold, there was a swarm of bees and honey in the carcass. He took some of the honey and brought it to his father and mother, who ate thereof.

A while later Samson married the Philistine woman and a great feast was held. At the celebration Samson put forth a riddle to the guests:

Out of the eater came forth food

And out of the strong came forth sweetness.

No one could give an answer to these words until his wife enticed it from him and then she told the guests:

That which is sweeter than honey and that

which is stronger than a lion.

Samson was displeased that his wife had given away the answer and went away for a time. While he was gone his father-in-law gave his wife to another man, supposing that Samson's heart had turned against her. When he returned, her father exhorted him that he take her fair younger sister instead, but he would not.

Now the ways and the customs of the Philistines were very different from those of the Israelites and on this account there was enmity and strife between the two peoples. Samson let loose foxes in the fields of the Philistines and burnt their crops and when they tried to capture him, he slew many of their number.

One day, he visited the city of Gaza and the Philistines made effort to seize him. He was still in the city when night came and the gates of the city were shut. It seemed as if he could not get out but he pulled down the doors of the gate of the city, the two posts, bar and all, put them on his shoulders and went off with them to the top of a hill near Hebron, that same place where Abraham was buried.

During all the twenty years that Samson was judge of the children of Israel, he discomforted the Philistines without ceasing so that they desired to make an end of him and they brought it about in this manner:

Samson loved a women whose name was Delilah and certain of the Philistines came to her and said, Entice Samson now, that we see where his great strength lies and we will give thee, everyone of us, eleven hundred pieces of silver.

Delilah was won over and asked Samson accordingly. He, making mock of her, said, "If I am tied up with seven green withes [flexible willow twigs], then is my strength the same as that of any other man."

She tied him up with seven green withes but he broke them as when a thread touches fire.

Again Delilah asked him, telling him not to mock her, and he said, "If I am tied up with new ropes then is my strength the same as that of any other man."

She tied him up with new ropes but he broke them like the withes.

Yet again Delilah asked him his secret and he said, "Weave the seven locks of my hair with the web of cloth on thy loom."

She did so and when Samson awoke, he rose up and the web with him.

Then Delilah asked him how he could love her, yet mock her and tell her lies, and Samson answered, "In truth my hair has never been shorn. From birth I was a Nazarite. If my head be shaven, then will my strength go from me."

Delilah saw that this time he made no mockery of her and she sent secretly for the Philistines, took their money and, while Samson slept, she called a man to shave off his locks.

When he awoke, he went out to shake himself as at other times before and the Philistines took him, put out his eyes and cast him into prison. Howbeit, the hair of his head began to grow again.

There came a time of feasting when the Philistines gathered together to make celebration and offer a sacrifice to their god, Dagon. When their hearts were merry, they called Samson and they made fun of him. They set him between the pillars of the temple which was full of people and which had three thousand persons on the roof.

As Samson stood in front of the building, he said to the lad which held his hand, "Let me feel the pillars whereon this house stands," and he cried: "O Lord God, Jehovah Elohim, remember me, I pray thee, and strengthen me only this once and let me die with the Philistines." He took hold of the two middle pillars on which the house stood, bowed himself with all his might and the house fell upon him and all that were therein, and thousands of Philistines perished. Then his brethren and all his father's household came down, took him away and buried him in the burying place of Manoah, his father.

THE BIRTH AND CHILDHOOD OF SAMUEL

At the time when Eli, the high priest, was judge of the children of Israel, there lived a good man called Elkanah and his wife, Hannah. Now Hannah was very grieved because she had no children and, entering the temple one day, she wept and prayed for a son. She vowed that if her wish were granted, the child would be devoted to the service of Jehovah and be brought up a Nazarite.

Hannah prayed silently and Eli marked her mouth. She spoke in her heart; her lips moved but her voice was not heard. Therefore Eli thought she was drunk and remonstrated with her; but Hannah replied, "Sire, I have drunk neither wine nor strong drink, but have poured out my soul before heaven, for I desire a son." Then Eli answered, "Go in peace and the God of Israel grant thee thy petition."

In the fullness of time Hannah bore a son and she called his name Samuel which means 'from God through prayer.'

74

While still a child he was taken by his mother to Eli, to serve in the temple, and he grew in favor both with Jehovah and with men. The word of Jehovah was precious in those days; there was no open vision.

Now Eli, the high priest, had two sons but they were wicked men and although Eli rebuked them with words, he did not correct their ways and they continued in unrighteousness. Eli grew old and his eyes were dim. One night when he had laid him down to sleep, with Samuel near him, Jehovah called: "Samuel." Samuel arose and ran to Eli, saying, "Here I am, for thou calledst me." But Eli said, "I called thee not, return to thy place." This came to pass a second time, for Samuel did not yet know Jehovah, neither was the word of Jehovah yet revealed unto him. A third time Jehovah called and Samuel again ran to Eli. Then Eli perceived who had called the child and he said to him, "Lie down now and if thou hearest the call again, say: 'Speak, Lord, for thy servant gives ear.'" So Samuel lay in his place and Jehovah called as at other times: "Samuel, Samuel," and Samuel answered as instructed by Eli, "Speak, Lord, for thy servant gives ear." Jehovah then told Samuel that because of the wickedness of Eli's sons and because Eli had not restrained them, the house of Eli would perish but that he, Samuel, would become judge.

THE ARK OF THE COVENANT IS CAPTURED

There was at that time strife again between the children of Israel and the Philistines and the Israelites went out against the Philistines to do battle. The Israelites had sinned and were smitten. They brought forth the Ark of the Covenant to the battlefield, hoping that this would help them to prevail, but the Philistines captured it. The Philistines put it in their temple next to their god, Dagon. In the morning they saw that Dagon had fallen on his face. They set him up again but, behold, the next morning he was lying on the floor with his head and his hands severed. Then the Philistines were sore afraid and sent the Ark to their neighbours but wherever the Ark came, the people were smitten with plagues. Therefore was the Ark returned quickly to the Israelites.

The sons of Eli had died in battle with the Philistines and when Eli died, on hearing of the death of his sons, Samuel became judge. He called together the people of Israel and exhorted them to serve only the god of Israel, and the Israelites hearkened unto him and were so strengthened that the Philistines were subdued all the days of Samuel.

THE ISRAELITES DEMAND A KING

When Samuel was old, he made his sons judges in Israel, but they walked not in his ways. They sought after lucre, took bribes: and perverted judgment. Then the elders of Israel came to him, saying, "Thy sons walk not in thy ways; now make us a king to judge us like other nations."

This thing displeased Samuel and he prayed to Jehovah for guidance and Jehovah said, "Hearken unto the voice of the people in all that they say unto thee; for they have not rejected thee but they have rejected me; yet show them the manner of the king that shall reign over them."

Samuel spoke to the people as instructed, saying, "This will be the manner of the king that shall reign over you: he will take your sons for his chariots and to be his horsemen, to sow his ground, to reap his harvest and to make his instruments of war. He will take your daughters to be cooks and to be bakers. He will take your fields and your vineyards and give them to his officers. He will take a tenth of your produce and sheep and you will be his servants."

Nevertheless the people said, "We will have a king over us that we may also be as other nations."

Samuel heard all the words of the people and rehearsed them in the ears of Jehovah and Jehovah answered, "Hearken unto their voice and make them a king."

THE STORY OF RUTH

A time of harmony and fulfilment

RUTH IN THE CORNFIELD

In the days when the judges ruled Israel, it came to pass that there was at one time a famine in the land. Therefore a certain man went to sojourn in the country of Moab, he and his wife, Naomi, and their two sons. There the man died. The two sons took wives of the women of Moab unto themselves but the sons also died. Therefore was Naomi bereft of them and her husband and there remained to her only Orpah and Ruth, her daughters-in-law.

When she heard that Jehovah had visited his people, giving them bread again, she went with her daughters-in-law to return to the land of Judah. Howbeit, she spoke to them, saying, "Perchance it is better that each of you return to her mother's house. Jehovah deal kindly with you as you have dealt with the dead and with me," and she turned to depart; but they wept and said, "Surely we will return with thee to thy people."

Naomi spoke again: "Go, my daughters, go your way. I am old and much grieved for your sakes and it is better you stay." Then Orpah kissed her mother, said farewell, and returned; but Ruth stayed with her, saying, "Whither thou goest, I will go; where thou lodgest, I will lodge; thy people shall be my people and thy god my god; where thou diest, there will I die and there will I be buried."

So Naomi and Ruth journeyed to Bethlehem and they came there at the time of the barley harvest. The people were moved and said, "Is this Naomi?" for she was much changed.

Now Naomi had a kinsman of her husband's, a mighty man of wealth, and his name was Boaz. He had fields of barley and Ruth went to glean ears of corn therein. Boaz came to visit his reapers and greeted them, saying, "Jehovah protect you," and they answered, "Jehovah bless thee." Then Boaz, seeing Ruth, said to his head servant, "Whose damsel is this?" and the servant answered, "It is the Moabite damsel that came back with Naomi out of the country of Moab whose story thou already knowest. She came and asked to glean among the sheaves."

Then Boaz said to Ruth, "Hear me, I pray thee. It has been shown to me all that thou hast done for thy mother-in-law and how thou hast returned here. Go not to glean in another field but abide here with my maidens. When thou art athirst, go to the vessels and drink, and at mealtimes eat of the bread with the reapers."

Ruth bowed and answered, "Let me find favor in thy sight, Sire, for that thou hast spoken kindly to thy handmaid," and she went away to continue with gleaning.

Boaz then commanded his young men to let fall some handsful of corn on purpose that Ruth might glean them.

In the evening she returned to her mother-in-law with a good measure of corn and gave tidings of Boaz and of her good fortune.

So Ruth gleaned in the fields until the end of the barley harvest and then until the end of the wheat harvest, and she found favor in the eyes of Boaz.

All the city knew that she was a virtuous woman and Boaz took her to wife. Jehovah blessed the marriage. Ruth bore a son and Naomi helped to nurse him, and he was called Obed. Obed was the father of Jesse and Jesse was the father of David, from whose line Jesus was born.

THE FIRST KINGS:
SAUL, DAVID, SOLOMON

The rise and fall of a kingdom

SAUL AND DAVID

There was a man of the tribe of Benjamin whose name was
Saul, a choice young man, and among the children of Israel there
was not a goodlier man than he. From his shoulders and upward
he was higher than any other man.

One day the asses of Saul's father were lost and Saul was sent
with one of the servants to search for them. After much wander-
ing they came to a city wherein they heard was a man of God.
This was Samuel. Now Jehovah had told Samuel in his ear a day
before Saul came, saying, "Tomorrow I will send thee a man out
of the tribe of Benjamin and thou shalt anoint him to be king over
my people Israel." Samuel met Saul and Jehovah said to him,
"Behold the man of whom I spoke," whereupon Samuel invited
Saul to eat with him and told him that the asses had been found.

On the morrow Samuel took a vial of oil, poured it upon the
head of Saul, kissed him and said, "Jehovah has anointed thee to
be king of his people," and he announced it to all the congregation of the Israelites, whereupon they shouted: "God save the
king."

So Saul became king. He did mighty deeds of valour and he
laid low the enemies of Israel but Saul also lusted after strange
gods whereby he became unfitted to rule.

Then Jehovah spoke to Samuel, saying, "It repents me that I
have set up Saul to be king, for he is turned back from following
me and has not performed my commandments. Go now to him
and tell him in my name that he is no longer fitted to be king.
Then go to Jesse, the Bethlehemite, for I have provided me a new
king from among his sons." Accordingly, Samuel journeyed to
Bethlehem, where Jesse caused seven of his sons to pass before
him. But Samuel said, "Jehovah has not chosen these. Are here all

thy children?," and Jesse answered, "No, not all, there remains yet the youngest and he is keeping the sheep."

"Send and fetch him, I pray thee," said Samuel, "for we will not sit down till he come hither." So David was sent for and he came. He was ruddy and withal of a beautiful countenance, goodly to look upon; and Jehovah said to Samuel, "Arise, anoint him for this is he." Then Samuel took the horn of oil and anointed David in the midst of his brethren, and the spirit of Jehovah hovered over David from that day forward. But these things were not yet known to Saul.

From Saul the protection of Jehovah had departed. An evil spirit troubled him and his servants said, "Let our master command us to seek out a man who is a cunning player on the harp that our master shall be well thereby." One of the servants then said, "Behold, I have seen a son of Jesse in Bethlehem who is a cunning player on the harp, prudent in matters and comely in person. Let him be sent for."

Therefore Saul sent a message unto Jesse, saying, "Send me, I pray thee, David, thy son, who is with the sheep, that he may ease my troubled spirit with the playing of the harp." So David came to Saul and stood before him. Saul came to love David greatly, made him his armour-bearer and when the evil spirit came upon him, David took his harp and played on it that Saul was refreshed and well, and the evil spirit departed from him.

DAVID CHALLENGES GOLIATH

Now the Philistines and the Israelites were again at enmity with one another and each gathered together their armies for battle. The Philistines stood on one mountain, the Israelites on another, with a valley between them.

From out of the army of the Philistines there came forth a champion, a man of huge stature, called Goliath. He had a helmet of brass upon his head; he was armed with a coat of mail; he had greaves of brass upon his legs and the staff of his spear was like a weaver's beam. He stood before the armies of Israel and cried unto them: "Choose a man from the armies of Israel to fight with me. If he kills me, then we will be your servants; but if I prevail against him, then shall you be our servants and serve us. I defy the armies of Israel. Give me a man that we may fight together."

When Saul and the Israelites heard these words, they were dismayed and greatly afraid.

Howbeit, among the Israelite men of war were the three eldest sons of Jesse and Jesse had said to his youngest son, David, "Take now this parched corn and these ten loaves and run to the camp to thy brethren; carry these ten cheeses to the captain of their thousand and look how thy brethren fare." So David had done as Jesse commanded him and visited his brethren. Now as he talked with them, behold, there came up the champion, Goliath, and spoke the same words as before. David heard them and enquired of their meaning. He then went before Saul and said, "Let no man's heart fail because of this Philistine; thy servant will go and fight with him," but Saul answered, "Nay, for thou art but a lad, and Goliath a man of war from his youth up."

David replied, "Thy servant kept his father's sheep and there came a lion and took a lamb out of the flock. I went out after him and smote him and delivered the lamb out of his mouth. Then came also a bear. Thy servant slew both lion and bear and this Philistine shall be as one of them."

Then was Saul reconciled and said to David, "Go, and heaven protect thee." He armed David with his own armor, put a helmet of brass upon his head and gave him a coat of mail but David said, ""I cannot go with these for I have not proved them" and he put them off. He took his staff and chose five smooth stones out of the brook and put them in his shepherd's bag. A sling was in his hand.

When the Philistine drew near and saw David, he disdained him and said, "Am I a dog that thou comest to me with staves? Come, and I will give thy flesh to the fowls of the air and to the beasts of the field."

David made answer: "Thou comest to me with a sword and a shield but I come to thee in the name of Jehovah, the god of the armies of Israel. This day will Jehovah deliver thee into my hand and I will smite thee."

He put a hand into his bag and took thence a stone. He put this in his sling, slung it and smote the Philistine in his forehead that he fell upon his face to the earth. So David prevailed but there was no sword in his hand. Therefore he ran, stood upon the Philistine, drew the Philistine's sword out of its sheath and cut off his head therewith.

When the Philistines saw that their champion was dead, they fled.

SAUL IS JEALOUS

After the death of Goliath there was much rejoicing among the congregation of the Israelites but Saul cast an envious eye on David because he was accorded the greater praise. An evil spirit came upon him and, in his anger, he cast a javelin at David, but David avoided out of his presence.

Saul then reasoned that David would be slain if he were in the forefront of battle and he promised David his daughter in marriage in exchange for the death of a hundred Philistines. It pleased David well to take Michal, Saul's daughter, to wife, but when he went to battle with the Philistines, Jehovah was with him and he received no hurt.

DAVID AND JONATHAN

Saul, being envious of David, spoke privily with his son and with his servants, to entice them to slay David; but Jonathan loved David as his own soul. They made a covenant together. Jonathan stripped himself of the robe that was upon him and gave it to David, also his garments, even to his sword, to his bow and to his girdle. Therefore when Saul spoke to Jonathan in this wise, Jonathan was grieved. He told David of the plot and exhorted him to stay in a secret place while he communed again with his father. Then Jonathan spoke good of David to Saul and

Saul hearkened unto him and repented of his evil thought. Moreover, he swore that he would do no more harm against David.

SAUL ATTACKS DAVID. DAVID SPARES HIS LIFE

Again there was war with the Philistines and the Philistines fled before David and his hosts. Saul was vexed at the praise which David received and the evil spirit came upon him. He sought to smite David again with the javelin but David slipped away out of Saul's presence and fled into the wilderness.

Saul's anger was kindled and he went with his servants to seek out David to slay him. It came to pass that David, trying to escape from his enemy, was hiding in a cave when Saul entered it to rest. Not perceiving that any person was there, Saul laid himself down to rest and fell asleep; therefore was he at the mercy of David but David withheld his hand. He cut off a portion of Saul's robe, which he showed him afterwards, thus proving that he had spared him and Saul repented once more. Then David went forth but he had no sooner gone than Saul's anger returned and he set forth again in pursuit.

Once David came to the place where Saul had pitched his camp. He entered by night and found Saul sleeping in his tent, with his spear and drinking cup beside him. David took the spear and the cup and no man saw him because Jehovah had caused a deep sleep to descend upon the camp. The next day David stood on the top of a hill afar off and cried to the people: "Now see where the king's spear is, and his drinking cup."

Saul knew David's voice and said, "Is this thy voice, my son David?" and David answered, "It is my voice, O king, my master. Wherefore does the king pursue after his servant, for what have I done, or what evil is in my hand?" Then said Saul, "I have sinned; return, my son David, for I will no longer do thee harm," but David went on his way.

SAUL AND JONATHAN DIE IN BATTLE

In a battle with the Philistines, Saul and his army could not prevail. Jonathan was slain and Saul wounded by the archers.

Then said Saul to his servant, "Draw thy sword and thrust me through therewith lest these Philistines come and slay me." But the servant would not, whereupon Saul took his own sword and fell on it.

A man out of the camp of Saul came to David, with his clothes rent and earth upon his head, and he bowed before David, saying, "Out of the camp of Israel am I escaped. The armies are fled, many are fallen. Saul and Jonathan, his son, are dead."

DAVID'S LAMENT

Then David lamented for Saul and Jonathan, crying:

The beauty of Israel is slain upon the high places;
    how are the mighty fallen!
Saul and Jonathan were lovely and pleasant in their
      lives, and in their death they were not divided. They
      were swifter than eagles; they were mightier than lions.
How are the mighty fallen in the midst of the battle! O
      Jonathan, thou wast slain in thy high places.
I am distressed for thee, my brother Jonathan. Very
      pleasant hast thy love been unto me. Thy love to me was
      wonderful, passing the love of women.
How are the mighty fallen, and the warriors perished!

DAVID BECOMES KING

There was a son of Saul who desired to follow in his father's place and there was strife between the house of Saul and the house of David; but the house of David waxed stronger and stronger and the house of Saul weaker and weaker. Then came all the tribes of Israel to David and spoke, saying, "Behold, we are thy bone and thy flesh. In times past when Saul was king over us, thou wast he who led us, and Jehovah was with thee. Be now king over all the people."

David listened, searched his heart and consented. Then he was anointed king but he remembered his love of Saul and Jonathan and showed mercy and did kindnesses to the members of their house yet living.

He was thirty years old when he began to reign and he reigned for forty years.

He subdued the Philistines, the Moabites, Syrians, Edomites, Ammonites, Amalekites and all that were enemies to Israel. He captured the castle of Zion by the city of Jerusalem and made his dwelling there. Therefore was it called the City of David.

He made affinity with Hiram, king of Tyre, who sent cedar trees, carpenters and masons, to build him a house.

At that time the Ark of the Covenant had no firm resting place and David gathered together all the chosen men of Israel and they brought it up and set it upon Mount Zion. Then the word of Jehovah came to Nathan the priest, saying, "Go and tell my servant David that he has built a house for himself but none for his god. He shall build a house for my name and I will establish the throne of his kingdom forever." So David began to make preparations according to the word of Jehovah through Nathan.

DAVID'S TRANSGRESSIONS

Then David did a thing which displeased Jehovah. He desired to know the number of his people. He sent word to Joab, the captain of his host and to the rulers of the people, "Go now, number Israel from Dan to Beersheba and bring the number that I may know it." Joab answered, "Wherefore does my lord require this thing? The people are all my lord's servants. Why will he intrude upon them?"

Nevertheless the king's word prevailed against Joab and Joab went through all Israel and gave the number to David, but of their welfare he did not enquire and the people became sick thereby. There was another thing which grieved Jehovah and that was David's desire for the wife of another.

It came to pass in an eveningtide that David walked on the roof of his house and saw a certain woman, very beautiful to look upon. He enquired after her and one said, "She is the wife of Uriah, the Hittite."

Then David sent a letter to the captain of his host, in which he wrote: "Set Uriah in the forefront of the hottest battle that he may be smitten and die." Soon thereafter came messengers to David saying, "Uriah is dead."

When the wife of Uriah heard that he was dead, she mourned exceedingly for him; but when the days of mourning were past, David sent and fetched her to his house and she became his wife.

Thereupon, Jehovah sent Nathan the prophet to David, and Nathan said unto him, "There were two men in one city. the one rich and the other, his servant, poor. The rich man had exceeding many flocks and herds; the servant had nothing save one little ewe lamb which grew up together with him and with his children. There came a traveler unto the rich man and he spared to take of his own flock to dress as meat for the wayfaring man; he took his servan''s lamb and dressed it for him that was come."

David's anger was greatly kindled against the rich man and he said, "As Jehovah lives, the man that has done this thing shall surely die because he did this thing and had no pity."

Then Nathan told him, "Thou art the man. Thus says the Lord God of Israel: I anointed thee king over Israel; I delivered thee out of the hand of Saul; I gave thee possession of Israel and Judah, yet thou hast killed Uriah the Hittite and hast taken his wife to be thy wife. Now therefore the sword shall never depart from thine house. Behold I will raise up evil against thee out of thine own house."

ABSALOM'S REBELLION AND DEATH

Now David had a son who was called Absalom. Absalom walked not in the way of Jehovah but in all Israel there was none to be so much praised for his beauty and the hair on his head. David loved him but would not see or converse with him because of his misdeeds.

Absalom sought to make himself loved by the people and he gathered men of war to himself to fight with the enemies of Israel against his father. There ensued a grievous battle wherein the Israelites triumphed. David had ordered his captains to deal gently with his son but, after the battle, Absalom fled from the field on the back of a mule. The mule ran under the thick boughs of a great oak and Absalom's head caught hold of the oak and he was taken up and suspended between heaven and earth. The mule that was under him went away.

This was told to the captain of the host of David who took three darts and thrust them through the heart of Absalom. He ordered that the body be taken down and cast into a great pit in the wood and a very great heap of stone be laid upon it.

Soon there came a man to David, crying: "Tidings, my Lord the King! Jehovah has avenged thee this day of all them that rose up against thee." Then the king asked, "Is the young man Absalom safe?" and the man answered, "He has perished with the others that rose against thee."

The king was much moved and wept, saying, "O my son Absalom, my son, my son, Absalom. Would that I had died for thee! O Absalom, my son, my son."

DAVID APPOINTS SOLOMON AS HIS SUCCESSOR

When David was old in years, there arose a dispute among his sons as to who should be king in his place. He called for the priest Zadok and the prophet Nathan and said to them, "Let my son Solomon be anointed king to rule in my place for I have appointed him."

Then he called for Solomon and charged him to build a house for the god of Israel. He spoke thus: "My son, it was in my mind to build a house unto the name of Jehovah, my god, but his word came to me saying: 'Thou hast shed blood abundantly and hast made great wars. Thou hast also done things which displeased me. Therefore shalt thou not build a house unto my name. Behold, a son shall be born to thee to whom I will give rest from all enemies round about and I will give peace and quietness to Israel in his days.' Now, my son, Jehovah be with thee. Prosper and build a house to his name. I have prepared talents of gold and silver, of brass and of iron, timber and stone. There are workers enough and all manner of cunning people for every kind of work."

These things David also told to the congregation of Israel, exhorting them to keep the commandments of Jehovah and to support Solomon in the building of the temple.

The days of David drew near that he should die. He charged his son Solomon, saying, "I go the way of all the earth; be thou strong and show thyself a man; keep the charge of Jehovah Elohim, to walk in his ways, to keep his statutes and his commandments, his judgments and his testimonies as it is written in the law of Moses, that thou mayest prosper in all that thou doest."

So David died in good old age, full of days, riches and honour, and he was buried in the city which bears his name.

SOLOMON BECOMES KING

After the death of David, Solomon became king and his kingdom was established greatly. He made affinity with Pharaoh, king of Egypt, took Pharaoh's daughter to wife and brought her into the city of David. Solomon walked in the ways of Jehovah and kept the statutes of David his father.

HE ASKS FOR WISDOM

It came to pass one night that Jehovah appeared to Solomon in a dream and, speaking for the Elohim, said to Solomon, "Ask what I shall give thee." Solomon answered, "O Lord my God, thou hast made thy servant king and I am but as a little child. Thy servant is in the midst of thy people, a great multitude which thou hast chosen. Give therefore thy servant an understanding heart to judge thy people, that I may discern between good and evil."

This speech pleased the Elohim and Jehovah answered, "Because thou hast asked this thing and has not asked for thyself long life, nor riches, nor for the life of thine enemies, behold I have done according to thy words. Lo, I have given thee a wise and understanding heart, so that there was none like thee before thee, neither after thee shall any arise like unto thee. I have also given thee that which thou hast not asked, both riches and honour. If thou wilt walk in my ways, keep my statutes and my commandments, then I will lengthen thy days."

As Jehovah had promised, Solomon had exceeding much understanding and largeness of heart, even as the sand that is on the seashore. His wisdom excelled the wisdom of all the children of the east country, and of Egypt.

He had knowledge of trees, from the Cedar of Lebanon to the Hyssop that springs out of the wall. He had knowledge of beasts and fowl and creeping things and fishes. In his lifetime he spoke three thousand proverbs and his songs were a thousand and five. There came people from all the kingdoms of the earth to hear his wisdom.

SOLOMON'S JUDGMENT

Soon after Solomon became king, there came two women unto him and stood before him. The one woman said, "O King, I and this woman dwell in one house and a child was born to each of us. There was no stranger in the house with us. This woman's child died in the night because she overlaid it and she arose at midnight, took my son from beside me while I slept, and laid the dead child in my bosom. When I rose in the morning and considered it, behold, it was not my son which I did bear."

The other woman then spoke, saying, "Nay, the living child is my son and the dead one hers."

The first woman answered, "The living son is mine. The dead is hers."

Thus they spoke before the king.

The king commanded that a sword be sent for.

When the sword was brought the king proclaimed: "Divide the child in two and give half to the one woman and half to the other."

Then cried the woman to whom the living child belonged: "Sire, I pray thee, give her the living child and in no wise slay it," but the other said, "Let it be neither mine nor thine but divide it."

The king spoke: "Give the first the living child, for she is the mother thereof."

All Israel heard of the judgment and they honored the king, for they saw that the wisdom of heaven was in him.

THE BUILDING OF THE TEMPLE

Hiram, King of Tyre, ever a lover of David, rejoiced greatly when Solomon became king; and Solomon sent to Hiram, saying, "Thou knowest how that my father could not build a house unto the Lord his God. Now I purpose to do it in his place. Command thou, therefore, I pray thee, that thy servants hew me cedar and fir trees out of Lebanon and my servants shall work with thy servants."

Hiram answered, "I have considered the things which thou askest and I will do all thy desire concerning timber of cedar and of fir."

Then Solomon gave to Hiram twenty-thousand measures of wheat for food to his household and twenty measures of pure oil, year by year. There was peace between Hiram and Solomon and they two made a league together.

Solomon raised a levy of thirty thousand men and he sent them, ten thousand at a time, to Lebanon. They spent a month in Lebanon and two months at home. He had three score and ten thousand laborers, four score thousand hewers in the mountains and three thousand and three hundred overseers.

The temple was built of stone made ready before it was brought to the site so that there was neither hammer nor axe nor any tool of iron heard in the house while it was being built. The walls of the house within were made with boards of cedar and the floor was covered with planks of fir. The cedar walls were carved with buds and open flowers. An inner room was prepared to house the Ark of the Covenant and it was lined with pure gold. The altar of cedar wood was also overlaid with gold.

Within this room were two Cherubim, made of olive wood, whose wings spanned the breadth of the room, and the Cherubim were overlaid with gold. The floor also was covered with gold. On the doors were carvings of Cherubim, palm trees and open flowers, and gold was fitted upon the carved work.

King Solomon sent and fetched Hiram out of Tyre. Hiram had wisdom and understanding in building and casting and he was a cunning worker in brass. For King Solomon he cast two pillars, finely decorated, and they were named Jachim and Boaz. He also made a molten sea, finely decorated, standing on twelve oxen of metal, and the brim thereof was like the brim of a cup but very great. Hiram also made all manner of vessels that pertained to that place.

When the temple was finished, Solomon assembled the elders of all Israel and all the heads of the tribes to Jerusalem that they might bring up the Ark of the Covenant. The elders came and the priests brought up the Ark of the Covenant into the temple which Solomon had built. In the Ark were the two tablets of stone which Moses had put there. When the priests had brought in the Ark and came forth, lo, a cloud filled the house and the cloud was the glory of Jehovah.

Then Solomon made speech before the altar and said, "Lord God of Israel, there is no god like thee in heaven or earth, but wilt thou indeed dwell on earth? Behold, the heaven and the heaven of heavens cannot contain thee; how much less this house that I have built! Yet have thou respect unto the cry and unto the prayer of thy servant and let this house be a place where thy people may make supplication unto thee. Moreover, if a stranger comes out of a far country for thy name's sake, when he shall pray in this house, hear thou in heaven, thy dwelling place."

Offerings were made and the king and all the children of Israel dedicated the temple.

In the fourth year of Solomon's reign was the foundation of the temple laid, and in the eleventh year was it finished. So was he seven years in building it.

SOLOMON'S PALACE AND OTHER WORKS

Then Solomon built a house for himself and was thirteen years in the building thereof. He made for himself a great throne of ivory and overlaid it with pure gold. On each side of the throne stood the figure of a lion and on each side of the steps leading to it, the figures of twelve lions. All his drinking vessels were of pure gold.

Solomon did also other famous works. He caused great cities to be built; he made a navy of ships; he changed the face of Jerusalem; he sent merchants to far distant parts who brought back gold, silver, spices, ivory, precious stones, apes and peacocks. He brought in horses and fine linen from Egypt.

THE VISIT OF THE QUEEN OF SHEBA

When the Queen of Sheba heard of the fame of Solomon, she came to test him with hard questions. She came to Jerusalem with a very great train, with camels that bore spices and very much gold and many precious stones. When she was come to Solomon, she communed with him of all that was in her heart and he answered all her questions, everything which she asked.

After the Queen has discerned the wisdom of Solomon, seen the house that he had built and the food at his table, seen the sitting of his servants, the attendance of his ministers and their apparel, his cupbearers also and their apparel, the ascent by which he went up to the temple, there was no more spirit in her. She said to the king, "It was a true report which I heard in mine own land of thine acts and of thy wisdom. Howbeit, I believed it not until I came. Behold the one half of the greatness of thy wisdom was not told to me for thou exceedest the fame that I heard. Happy are thy servants which stand before thee and hear thy wisdom."

The queen gave the king much gold, spices of great value, precious stones, and the king gave her all her desire, whatsoever she asked, as well as of his royal bounty. So she turned and went to her own country, she and her servants.

SOLOMON WORSHIPS FALSE GODS AND DIES

King Solomon loved many foreign women and when he grew old, his wives turned his thoughts towards other gods. His heart was not perfect with the Lord his God. He did evil in the sight of Jehovah, wherefore Jehovah said unto him, "Forasmuch as thou hast not kept my covenant, I will rend the kingdom from thee. Notwithstanding, I will not do it in thy days for thy father's sake but will rend it out of the hand of thy son."

Solomon died and slept with his fathers. He was buried in the city of David, and Rehoboam, his son, reigned in his stead.

THE KINGDOM IS DIVIDED

When Rehoboam became king, the whole people of Israel came to him and demanded that their tasks be made lighter but Rehoboam would not grant their desire. Then ten of the tribes rose up in rebellion against him and made Jeroboam king of their ten tribes in his stead. Jeroboam was a mighty man of valour and a son of one of Solomon's servants. Rehoboam remained king of the other two tribes, Benjamin and Judah, and dwelt in Jerusalem.

Thus the children of Israel were divided into two nations. The ten tribes of the north kept the name Israel but the kingdom of the south, under Rehoboam, was called Judah.

There arose strife between the two kingdoms. Israel and Judah fought one another and both neglected the laws of Jehovah.

There were now two kingdoms in the land of Canaan. The northern kingdom was called Israel, and its people Israelites, while the kingdom of the south was called Judah, and its peoples, Jews.

The Israelites continued to do evil in the sight of the Lord. They yielded unto wickedness and unto heathen gods and heeded not the words of the prophets which the Lord Jehovah sent to call them to repentance. Therefore Jehovah stirred up the Assyrians and sent them to descend upon the land. They laid seige to Samaria, the chief city of the Israelites, and subdued it after three years. The chiefs and the leaders of the Israelites were taken away captive into Assyria and they that were taken returned not again to their own country. The Assyrians brought strange peoples into the land and they mingled with those left behind. Thus the kingdom of Israel was no more and the peoples dwelling there were called by other names. Those who dwelt by the Sea of Galilee were called Galileans and those around the city of Samaria were called Samaritans.

For a season the people of Judah followed the way of Jehovah but they too began to follow false gods, whereupon affliction descended upon them.

THE PROPHETS:
ELIJAH, ELISHA, ISAIAH & OTHERS

The call to repentance. The coming Messiah

ELIJAH'S MISSION AND JOURNEYS

At one time a king called Ahab ruled over Israel and he did evil in the sight of Jehovah. His wife, Jezebel, worshipped Baal and she caused Ahab to raise up an altar to him. The evil that they did was above all that were before them. Therefore Jehovah sent his prophet to admonish them.

This prophet was a man of God called Elijah, and Elijah said to Ahab, "As the Lord God of Israel liveth, before whom I stand, there shall be no dew nor rain in this land these years for reason of thy wickedness, except according to my word."

When he had spoken thus, the word of Jehovah came to him, saying, "Get thee hence and hide thyself by the brook, Cherith. Thou shalt drink of the brook and I have commanded ravens to feed thee." Elijah did accordingly. Howbeit, the brook dried up and the word of Jehovah came again to him, saying, "Arise, get thee to Zarephath and dwell there. Behold I have commanded a widow woman there to sustain thee." So he arose and went to Zarephath. When he came to the gate of the city, a widow woman was there gathering sticks. He called to her and said, "Fetch me, I pray thee, a little water in a vessel that I may drink; bring also a morsel of bread in thy hand."

She answered Elijah: "As the Lord thy God liveth, I have but a handful of meal in a barrel and a little oil in a cruse. I am gathering sticks that I may prepare a last bite for me and my son, eat it and then die."

But Elijah said, "Fear not. Make me a little cake and one for thee and one for thy son. Thus says the Lord God of Israel: 'The barrel of meal shall not waste, neither shall the cruse of oil fail, until the day that Jehovah shall send rain upon the earth.'" The widow went and did according to the words of Elijah and the barrel of meal wasted not, neither did the cruse fail and her household did eat many days.

After these things the son of the woman fell sick and she said to Elijah, "O thou man of God, art thou come to call my sin to remembrance and to slay my son?" Elijah took the child, carried him up into a loft and laid him upon his own bed. He cried unto Jehovah and said, "O Lord my God, let this child's soul come again into him," and the child revived.

After many days the word of Jehovah came again to Elijah: "Go, show thyself unto Ahab and I will send rain upon the earth."

CONTEST WITH THE PRIESTS OF BAAL

So Elijah stood before Ahab and Ahab said to him, "Art thou he that troubles Israel?" but Elijah answered, "I have not troubled Israel but thou and thy father's house in that thou hast forsaken the commandments of Jehovah and hast followed after false gods. Now therefore gather all Israel unto Mount Carmel and the prophets of Baal, four hundred and fifty, that we may witness who is god."

So Ahab sent unto all the children of Israel and gathered his prophets together at Mount Carmel accordingly.

Elijah came and spoke to the people, saying, "If Jehovah be god, follow him; but if Baal, then follow him. I, even I alone, remain a prophet of Jehovah but the prophets of Baal number four hundred and fifty. Let us take two bullocks, one for the prophets of Baal, one for myself. Let the prophets of Baal prepare one bullock for sacrifice, put it on wood but lay no fire under it. I will do likewise. Then shall the prophets of Baal call on the name of their god and I will call on the name of mine. The one that answers by fire, let him be god."

The prophets of Baal took their bullock, dressed it and called upon the name of Baal from morning until noon but there was no voice nor answer.

At noon, Elijah mocked them, saying, "Cry louder. Either your god is talking, or hunting, or on a journey, or peradventure he is sleeping and must be awakened." Then they cried louder and cut themselves with knives after their fashion but there was no voice nor answer.

In the evening Elijah said to the people, "Come near." He took twelve stones and built an altar. He made a trench about the altar. He put wood on the altar and the offering on the wood. He called for barrels of water to be poured over the offering, a first time, a second time and a third time. Then he said, "Jehovah Elohim, Lord God of Abraham, Isaac and Jacob, let it be known this day that thou are God."

Thereupon fire fell from heaven and consumed the sacrifice, the wood, the stones, the dust, and licked up the water that was in the trench.

When the people saw this, they fell on their faces and cried: "Jehovah, he is God. Jehovah he is God," and they rose up and slew the prophets of Baal.

Elijah went to the top of the mount with his servant and said to him, "Look towards the sea." The servant looked but said, "There is nothing." Seven times Elijah told him to look and at the seventh time he said, "Behold, there ariseth a little cloud out of the sea, like a man's hand." Then did the heaven become black with clouds and wind and there was a great rain.

ELIJAH FLEES FROM JEZEBEL'S WRATH

Ahab told Jezebel all that Elijah had done and she, in her wrath, sought to have him killed. Therefore Elijah fled and went into the wilderness where he sat down under a juniper tree, saying, "It is enough; now O Lord, take away my life, for I am not better than my fathers." He fell asleep and as he slept, the Archangel Michael touched him and said, "Arise and eat." He opened his eyes and behold, there was a cake and a cruse of water before him. So he did eat and drink and laid him down again. The Archangel Michael came a second time, touched him and said, "Arise and eat." So he arose and did eat and drink and went in the strength of that food forty days and forty nights until he came to Horeb, the holy mount. Thither he came to a cave and lodged in it. There the word of Jehovah came to him to go forth and stand upon the mount before him.

Then behold! Jehovah passed by and a great strong wind rent the mountains and broke the rocks in pieces but Jehovah was not in the wind. After the wind came an earthquake but Jehovah was not in the earthquake; after the earthquake was a fire but Jehovah was not in the fire, and after the fire, a still, small voice.

When Elijah heard it, he wrapped his face in his mantle and went out and stood at the entrance of the cave and Jehovah said, "Go, return on thy way to the wilderness of Damascus. Anoint Hazael to be king over Syria and Jehu to be king over Israel, for these two are evil and shall destroy one another that the earth be cleansed of them. Anoint also Elisha, the son of Shaphat, to be my prophet after thee."

So Elijah departed and did accordingly. He found Elisha ploughing with twelve yoke of oxen before him and Elijah cast his mantle upon him. Thereupon Elisha left his ploughing and ran after him to minister unto him.

NABOTH'S VINEYARD

Now there was a vineyard hard by the palace of Ahab and when Elijah was not forth at Jehovah's behest, he tarried there as one with a different countenance and was called Naboth. Ahab desired to purchase the vineyard to add to his own garden but Naboth would not sell the inheritance of his fathers. Thus Ahab was heavy and displeased. He laid him down upon his bed, turned away his face and would eat no bread.

Jezebel came to him and asked, "Why is thy spirit so sad?" and when he had told her what was in his heart, she answered, "Let thy spirit be merry; I will get thee this vineyard," and Ahab gave her leave to do as she desired.

Now Jezebel was a sorceress and she had divined Naboth's secret. She saw the way to avenge the death of the prophets of Baal. She wrote letters in Ahab's name, sealed them with his seal and sent them to the elders of the city. She wrote: "Let two men be found who will bear witness against Naboth that he blasphemes god and king. Then let him be found guilty. Carry him out and stone him that he may die."

The elders of the city received the writing with the king's seal and did as Jezebel commanded; then they sent a message to her saying, "Naboth is dead."

When Jezebel heard this, she said to Ahab, "Arise, take possession of the vineyard which thou desirest, for Naboth is dead."

So Ahab went into the vineyard to take possession of it and there came towards him the spirit of Naboth-Elijah who spoke thus: "Hast thou killed and also taken possession? In the place where dogs licked the blood of Naboth shall dogs lick thy blood. Dogs shall eat Jezebel by the wall of Jezreel. Thou hast sold thyself to work evil in the sight of Jehovah, thou and thy wife; therefore shall thy house be utterly destroyed."

Ahab trembled exceedingly and was sore afraid, for he perceived now that Elijah and Naboth were one and when he heard those words, he rent his clothes, put sackcloth on his flesh, fasted and went softly.

In the fulness of time the things of which Elijah had spoken came to pass.

ELIJAH IS CARRIED TO HEAVEN IN A WHIRLWIND

The time came for the spirit of Elijah to ascend unto heaven and Elisha communed with him. Together they crossed the Jordan and Elijah said unto Elisha, "Ask what I shall do for thee before I be taken away from thee," and Elisha answered, "I would that thy spirit continue to live within me like a second self."

As they parted there appeared a chariot of fire and horses of fire and parted them asunder and Elisha saw Elijah carried by a whirlwind into heaven. It seemed to Elisha that Elijah's mantle fell from him and descended upon himself. He beheld the soul of Elijah and cried: "Father, sun-hero and genius of the people of Israel."

When Elisha's disciples met him, they said, "The spirit of Elijah does rest on Elisha," and they came to him and bowed themselves to the ground before him.

ELISHA PERFORMS WONDERS

Many were the deeds of Elisha on whom the mantle of Elijah had fallen.

When he was in Jericho, the people of the city came to him and said, "Behold, the situation of this city is pleasant but the water is naught and the ground barren." Thereupon Elisha demanded a cruse with some salt therein and he went forth to the spring of the waters and did cast in the salt. So the waters were healed until this day.

There was war between the Israelites and the Moabites and the Israelites went forth to fight but there was no water in the land. Elisha prayed unto Jehovah for succour and lo, the rains came and the ditches were filled.

A certain widow was hard pressed because she was in debt and had not the wherewithal to pay her creditor. Elisha came to her and asked what she had in the house, and the woman answered, "Only a tiny pot of oil." Elisha told her to borrow empty vessels of her neighbours, all that she could, and to pour from the small pot into them. Vessel after vessel was filled and Elisha said, "Go; sell the oil, pay thy debts and live thou and thy children from the money left over."

It fell on a day that Elisha passed to Shunem where there was a rich woman who constrained him to eat bread. As often as he came that way he turned in thither. One day the woman said to her husband, "Let us make a little room at the top of the house, set there a bed, a table, a stool, and a candlestick, and it shall be that when Elisha comes to us he shall turn in thither." Now the woman was without child and was astounded when Elisha prophesied to her that she would bear a son.

When the child was grown, it happened that he went out to his father in the field, to the reapers, where he fell sick and cried:

"My head, my head." He was taken home and sat on his mother's knees till noon, then died.

Now Elisha was not in the house at that time but the woman straightway saddled an ass and rode to Mount Carmel to seek him. He saw her coming towards him and knew that her soul was troubled because of the child.

He returned with the woman and went up to the room where the child lay on the bed. He touched his mouth and eyes, stretched himself upon the child and the flesh of the child waxed warm. He walked to and fro, stretched himself again upon the child, who sneezed seven times and opened his eyes.

When the woman was called in, Elisha said, "Take up thy son," and the woman fell at his feet, bowed herself to the ground, took up her son and went.

Elisha was in Gilgal and there was famine in the land. His disciples were sitting before him and he bade his servant: "Set on the great pot and see the pottage." One man went out into the field to gather herbs and he brought and shred them into the pot but he knew them not. As the men tasted the pottage they cried out: "O thou man of God, there is death in the pot." Then Elisha said, "Bring meal," and he cast it into the pot, whereupon the pottage became wholesome and there was no harm in it.

NAAMAN'S LEPROSY

Now Naaman, captain of the host of the king of Syria, was a great man, honourable, a mighty man of valour, but a leper. There was in his house a little Israelite maid who waited on his wife and she spoke to her mistress concerning the prophet of Israel and his power to heal.

This thing was told to Naaman; so he took his horses and his chariot and came and stood at the door of Elisha's house and Elisha sent a messenger to him, saying, "Go and wash in Jordan seven times and thy flesh shall come again to thee, and thou shalt be clean."

Then was Naaman wroth, saying, "Are not the rivers of Syria better than the waters of Israel. May I not wash in them and be clean!" So he turned and went away in a rage; but his servants came near and said, "Master, if the prophet had bid thee do some great thing, wouldest thou not have done it? How much rather then when he says: Wash and be clean!"

Naaman repented, went down to the river, dipped himself seven times in Jordan and his flesh came again like the flesh of a little child and he was clean.

He returned to Elisha and said, "Behold, I know now that there is no god in all the earth but in Israel. Take, I pray thee, some present from me," but Elisha would have none, saying to Naaman, "Go in peace."

So Naaman departed but Gehazi, Elisha's servant, thought to himself, "Behold my master has cured this Syrian but has taken nothing from him. I will run after him and take somewhat of him." So he followed after Naaman and when he had come up with him, he said, "My master sent me to ask for two talents of silver and two changes of raiment for two of his disciples which have even come to him." With a glad heart Naaman gave him the talents and the raiment and Gehazi returned and hid them, then stood before his master.

Elisha asked, "Whence comest thou, Gehazi?" and Gehazi answered, "No whither."

Then Elisha said, "My heart tells me what thou hast done. Is it a time to receive money or to receive garments? Thou has transgressed and the leprosy of Naaman shall therefore descend on thee." Thus Gehazi went forth out of his presence a leper.

ELISHA'S POWER AND KNOWLEDGE

It fell on a day that the disciples of Elisha came to him, saying, "The place where we live is too narrow. Let us go, we pray thee, to Jordan, cut down trees and make ourselves a habitation there."

Elisha concurred and as one man was felling a tree, the axe-head fell into the water and he cried: "Alas master," for it was borrowed.

Elisha asked where it fell, cut down a stick and threw it into the water. Then did the iron swim on the surface of the water and the man put forth his hand and took it.

In those days the king of Israel warred against Syria and took counsel with his servants, saying, "In such and such a place shall be my camp," but Elisha warned him to avoid that place because the Syrians knew it.

Twice was the king of Israel saved by a message from Elisha and the king of Syria was wroth. Then one of his servants said, "This thing lies with Elisha, the prophet of Israel, who tells the king of Israel the words that thou speakest in thy room."

Then the king of Syria sent his horsemen and his chariots to capture Elisha and they surrounded him. When Elisha saw that the Syrians were all around him, he prayed to Jehovah that they might be smitten with blindness, and Jehovah heard. Elisha then led them to the city of the king of Israel where their eyes were opened. The king of Israel desired to destroy the Syrians but Elisha commanded that they be given food and drink and sent away. So the bands of Syria came no more into the land of Israel.

DEATH OF ELISHA

Now Elisha was fallen sick and Joash, king of Israel at that time, came down unto him and wept over him, saying, "Father, father, sun-hero and genius of Israel," and Elisha said to him, "Take bow and arrows; put thy hand upon the bow." Then Elisha placed his hands upon the king's hands and said, "Shoot." Joash shot the arrow and Elisha cried: "The arrow of deliverance," and so died.

He was buried in a sepulchre and it came to pass that a band of Moabites invaded the land and they cast a dead man into the sepulchre; but when the dead man touched the bones of Elisha, behold, the dead man revived and stood upon his feet.

Now the word of Jehovah came to Jonah, saying, "Arise, go to Nineveh, that great city, and cry against it, for its wickedness is come up before me." But Jonah fled from the presence of Jehovah and went down to Joppa where he found a ship going to Tarshish. So he paid his fare and sailed with it.

Then Jehovah sent out a great wind and there was a mighty tempest in the sea so that the ship was likely to be broken. The mariners were afraid and every man cried unto his god. They cast forth the wares that were in the ship to lighten it but Jonah had gone below and he lay fast asleep.

The shipmaster came to him and said, "What means this, O sleeper! Call upon thy god that we perish not."

Then the mariners spoke among one another, saying, "Come, let us cast lots that we may know who has caused this evil to come upon us." So they cast lots and the lot fell upon Jonah.

They said to him, "Tell us, we pray thee, what is thine occupation? Whence comest thou! What is thy country? Of what people art thou? Why art thou aboard this ship?"

Jonah answered, "I am a Hebrew; I fear Jehovah and I have fled from his presence."

Then said they unto him, "What shall we do unto thee that the sea may be calm?" for it was tempestuous; and he answered them, "Cast me forth into the sea, for I know that I am the cause why this great tempest is upon you."

Nevertheless, the men rowed hard to bring the ship to land but they could not; wherefore they cried unto Jehovah: "We beseech thee, O Lord, let us not perish for this man's transgression and lay not innocent blood upon us." So they took Jonah, cast him into the sea and the sea ceased from her raging.

Now Jehovah had prepared a great fish to swallow up Jonah and he was in the belly of the fish three days and three nights. There Jonah prayed unto the Lord his God and acknowledged his great power and might. Then Jehovah spoke to the fish and it vomited Jonah out on to the dry land.

There the word of Jehovah came unto Jonah the second time, saying, "Arise; go unto Nineveh, that great city, and preach unto it the preaching that I bid thee."

So Jonah arose and went unto Nineveh and he announced: "Yet forty days and Nineveh shall be overthrown."

NINEVEH REPENTS

The people of Nineveh heard him, believed and repented. They proclaimed a fast and put on sackcloth, from the greatest of them unto the least. The king caused a proclamation to be made throughout all Nineveh, which said, "Let people turn from evil ways and from violence. Who can tell if the heavenly powers will not relent and turn away from fierce anger, that we perish not."

The people hearkened and turned from their evil ways. Thus the destruction which had been threatened through the mouth of Jonah came not upon them.

Then was Jonah displeased exceedingly. He was very angry because his prophecy was not fulfilled and he prayed to Jehovah to take his life; but Jehovah said, "Doest thou well to be angry, Jonah?" Jonah went and sat on the east side of the city where he made him a booth and sat under it in the shadow till he might see what would become of the city.

Jehovah Elohim prepared a gourd and made it come up over Jonah that it might be a shadow over his head. So Jonah was exceeding glad of the gourd; but a worm came when the morning rose next day and it smote the gourd that it withered. There came also a vehement east wind and when the sun beat upon the head of Jonah, he fainted and wished to die.

Then the Elohim said, "Doest thou well to be angry because the gourd withered?" and Jonah answered, "I do well to be angry," and Jehovah said, "Thou sorrowest for the gourd, for that which thou hast not laboured, neither madest it grow, which came up in a night and perished in a night; and should I not spare Nineveh, that great city, wherein are more than six score thousand persons, and also much cattle?"

ISAIAH PREACHES TO THE PEOPLE

The wickedness of the people of Judah became great, and the prophet Isaiah exhorted them to repentance, saying, "Hear, O heavens, and give ear, O earth, for Jehovah speaks: 'I have nourished and brought up children and they have rebelled against me. They are a sinful nation, a people laden with iniquity, a seed of evil doers and corrupters. They have forsaken me; they have provoked the Holy One of Israel into anger with their abominations.' Say now to my people: 'Come now, let us reason together; though your sins be as scarlet, they shall be as white as snow; though they be red like crimson, they shall be as wool. If you be willing and obedient, you shall eat the good of the land, but if you refuse and rebel, you shall be devoured with the sword.'

"The destruction of the transgressors and of the sinners shall be together and they that forsake Jehovah shall be consumed. Wash you, make you clean, put away the evil of your doings, cease to do evil, learn to do well, seek wisdom, relieve the oppressed, help the fatherless, plead for the widow. Learn to see, hear and understand.

Woe unto them that seek to possess the earth.

Woe unto them that rise up early in the morning to take strong drink until evening.

Woe unto them that praise themselves for their wickedness.

Woe unto them that call evil, good, and good, evil.

Woe unto them that are wise in their own eyes.

Woe unto them that decree unrighteous decrees.

Woe unto the inhabitants of Judah who shall be led away into captivity, even though a remnant of them return."

PROPHECY CONCERNING THE COMING OF CHRIST

But Isaiah also prophesied the coming of the savior, saying, "Unto us a child shall be born, unto us a son be given, and the government shall be upon his shoulder. His name shall be called Wonderful, Counsellor, The Mighty God, The Everlasting Father, The Prince of Peace.

"He shall come forth from the stem of Jesse and the spirit of Jehovah shall rest upon him, the spirit of wisdom and understanding, the spirit of counsel and of might, the spirit of knowledge and of the fear of Jehovah.

"He shall be born from among the remnant of Judah and that people shall make ready to receive him."

HEZEKIAH STRUGGLES AGAINST THE ASSYRIANS

In the days of the prophet Isaiah there reigned a king in Judah whose name was Hezekiah. He was twenty-five years old when he began to reign and he did that which was right in the sight of Jehovah. He removed the high places, destroyed the images and cut down the groves. He trusted Jehovah, the Lord God of Israel, and kept his commandments and Jehovah was with him. He smote the Philistines and defied the Assyrians.

In the fourteenth year of his reign the king of Assyria came up against the fenced cities of Judah and with a great host set down before Jerusalem. He made a proclamation to the Jews in the city with the words: "Let not Hezekiah deceive you. He will say that your Lord God will deliver you but it will not be. This city shall be delivered into my hands. Come now forth and make agreement with me." But the people held their peace.

When word of the proclamation was brought to King Hezekiah, he rent his clothes and sent messengers unto Isaiah to seek counsel.

Isaiah answered, "Thus says Jehovah: 'Be not afraid of the words which the king of Assyria has spoken and which have blasphemed me. I will send a blast upon him and he shall return to his own land and fall by the sword.'"

In the meantime the king of Assyria sent a letter to Hezekiah, in which he wrote: "Let not thy god deceive thee. Thou hast heard what the kings of Assyria have done to other lands and peoples. Their gods have not delivered them from our hands, neither will your god deliver you."

Hezekiah received the letter, read it, went into the house of prayer and said, "O Lord God of Israel, which dwellest between

107

the Cherubim, bow down thine ear and hear; open Lord, thine eyes and see the words of Sennacherib, king of Assyria. Of a truth, Lord, the kings of Assyria have destroyed the nations and their lands and have cast their gods into the fire, for they were no gods but the work of men's hands, wood and stone. Therefore they have destroyed them. Now, therefore, Jehovah Elohim, O Lord our God, I beseech thee, save us out of the hands of the Assyrians that all the kingdoms of the earth may know that thou art the Lord God, even thou only."

THE ASSYRIAN ARMY IS DESTROYED

Then Isaiah sent to Hezekiah, and said unto him, "Thus says the Lord God of Israel: that which thou hast prayed to me against Sennacherib, king of Assyria, I have heard. He shall not come into this city, nor shoot an arrow there, nor come before it with shield, nor lay siege to it."

That night the Archangel Michael went out and smote in the camp of the Assyrians a hundred and four score and five thousand men. When Sennacherib arose early in the morning, behold, there were dead corpses all around him. So he departed and returned to Nineveh and there he was slain by the swords of his sons.

HEZEKIAH'S SICKNESS AND RECOVERY

In those days was Hezekiah sick unto death, Isaiah came to him and said, "Set thine house in order for thou art about to die." Then Hezekiah turned his face to the wall and prayed unto Jehovah: "I beseech thee, O Lord, remember how I have walked before thee in truth and with a perfect heart and have done that which is good in thy sight," and he wept sore.

As Isaiah left the house, Jehovah spoke to him: "Turn again and tell Hezekiah, the captain of my people, that I have heard his prayer and will heal him. I will add unto his days fifteen years and as a sign of my covenant the shadow of the sun dial shall go back ten degrees."

So Hezekiah was healed and he amassed much riches, built cities, made reservoirs and built a conduit to bring water into Jerusalem.

The son of the king of Babylon heard that Hezekiah had been sick and sent him letters and a present and came to visit him with his servants. Hezekiah welcomed them and showed them all his precious things, his silver, gold, costly spices, precious ointment and all the house of his armor. There was nothing in his house nor in his whole dominion that Hezekiah showed them not, and they departed full of wonder.

Then came Isaiah to Hezekiah and was wroth that all these things were shown to the men of Babylon and he said, "Behold the days will come when all that is in thine house shall be carried away into Babylon, thy sons also." But Hezekiah answered, "Good is the word that thou hast spoken. Is it not good if there is peace and truth in my days?"

So Hezekiah died and all Judah and the inhabitants of Jerusalem did honour him at his death.

THE BABYLONIAN CAPTIVITY:
JEREMIAH, EZEKIEL, DANIEL

The dark hour before the dawn

JEREMIAH REMONSTRATES WITH THE PEOPLE

Jehovah now called upon Jeremiah, the son of a priest, to be his mouthpiece and told him to say to the people,"Thus says Jehovah: 'Why have you forgotten me, who brought you out of the land of Egypt, who led you through the wilderness, who brought you into a land flowing with milk and honey? Now have you defiled my land and made my heritage an abomination. Turn, O backsliding children, and I will feed you with knowledge and understanding.'"

But the wicked prospered and they who dealt treacherously were seemingly happy and Jeremiah made complaint over these things to Jehovah; he declared that men reviled him for calling them to repentance but Jehovah urged him to continue to preach.

Therefore he spoke to the people unceasingly until a certain priest grew weary of his speaking and found cause to arrest him. Then was Jeremiah put in the stocks for the night by the upper gate of the city.

HE FORETELLS THE COMING CAPTIVITY OF THE JEWS AND ALSO THE COMING OF CHRIST

The next morning he was released and he continued to prophesy. In the name of Jehovah he prophesied that the Jews would be taken into captivity for seventy years. He also announced the coming of the Messiah, saying, "Thus says Jehovah: 'Behold the days will come that I will raise unto David a righteous branch; a king shall reign and prosper and shall execute judgment and justice in the earth.'"

Again Jeremiah was arrested but his enemies were loath to hold him when he appealed to the people that he spoke in the name of Jehovah. He continued to preach destruction and repentance.

Then certain of the princes were wroth against Jeremiah and cast him into prison and there he remained until the Babylonians took the city. The king of Babylon knew that Jeremiah had spoken truthfully and released him and gave him leave to live wherever he so desired. He was taken by some of his people to Egypt and there he died.

EZEKIEL'S VISIONS, DESCRIBED BY HIMSELF

Now it came to pass that I, Ezekiel, was among the first of the captives to be taken from Judah to Babylon.

One day, as I stood with other captives by the river, the heavens opened themselves to me and I saw a vision of heavenly powers. I looked and behold, a whirlwind came out of the north, a great cloud and a fire within it, and about it a great brightness. Out of the midst thereof came the likeness of four living creatures. Every creature had four faces and four wings. To the front their faces were like the faces of men; to the right like those of a lion; to the left, of an ox; and to the rear, of an eagle. Their wings were stretched upward and the likeness of the firmament was above them and above the firmament the likeness of a throne. On the throne was a figure in the likeness of a man and round about was brightness like the bow in the cloud in the day of rain. This was the appearance of the likeness of the glory of Jehovah. When I saw it, I fell on my face and I heard the voice of one that spoke. He said unto me, "Son of Man, go to the children of Israel who rebel against me. Be not afraid. Say to the people that I have seen their iniquity and that their transgressions will be visited upon them; yet will I take a remnant of them back to their own land and sprinkle clean water upon them and put new spirit into them."

The hand of Jehovah came upon me and carried me out in spirit and set me down in the midst of a valley of dry bones. Then Jehovah said to me, "Can these bones live?" I answered, "O Lord

God, thou knowest." He said to me, "Prophesy upon these bones and say: 'Jehovah shall cause breath to enter into you and you shall live.'" So I prophesied as commanded and there was a great noise of bones coming together. As I looked, sinews and flesh came upon them and skin covered them but there was no breath in them.

Then he said to me, "Say to the winds in my name that they shall breathe upon these slain that they may live." So breath came into them, and spirit, and they lived and stood upon their feet, an exceeding great army.

Jehovah spoke again: "These bones are the house of Israel. Say to them in my name that I will put my spirit into them and they shall live and that I shall put them in their own land."

Thereafter, being a priest and open to the word of Jehovah, I set out the rules by which priests and people should live.

DANIEL AT THE COURT OF THE KING OF BABYLON

The might of Babylon was now great and the Israelites who had dwelt in Judah had now been taken into Babylon into captivity. The king of Babylon, Nebuchadnezzar, ordained that certain children of the captives be chosen to serve at his court. They had to be children in whom was no blemish, who were well-favoured, skillful in all wisdom, cunning in knowledge, understanding in science, and such as had ability to stand in the king's palace and learn the wisdom and the tongue of the Chaldeans. The king appointed them a daily provision of his food and of the wine which he drank, so nourishing them three years that at the end they might stand before the king.

Among those chosen were Daniel, Hananiah, Meshael and Azariah, but the chief chamberlain gave them new names, Belteshazzar, Shadrach, Meshach and Abednego.

Belteshazzar, that is, Daniel, purposed in his heart that he would not eat of the king's food nor drink of his wine and requested the king's chamberlain that he and his friends might abstain; but the chief chamberlain said unto Daniel, "I fear my master, the king, will see your faces worse looking than the other children of your sort and that will cost me my head." Howbeit, the chief chamberlain was well disposed and friendly towards Daniel and Daniel said, "Prove us, I beseech thee, for ten days. Let our food contain no flesh and give us water to drink. Then look upon our countenances and compare them with the countenances of the others."

The chief chamberlain consented in this matter and lo, at the end of ten days the countenances of these four appeared fairer and fatter in flesh than those of all the children which did eat the portion of the king's food.

To these four the heavenly powers gave also knowledge and skill in all learning and wisdom, and Daniel had understanding in all visions and dreams. When they were brought in before the king, the king communed with them and found none like them. In all matters of wisdom and understanding that the king enquired of them, he found them ten times better than all the magicians and astrologers that were in his realm.

THE KING'S DREAMS

In the second year of his reign Nebuchadnezzar had a dream and his spirit was troubled. He commanded his magicians, astrologers and sorcerers to attend on him and said, "I have dreamed a dream and my spirit is troubled to know the dream. Tell me therefore what I have dreamed and the interpretation thereof."

The chief of the wise men spoke: "O King, live forever. Tell thy servants the dream and we will show the interpretation."

Howbeit, the king answered, "The thing is gone from me. Make you known the dream unto me," but they could not.

Now the secret of this thing had been revealed to Daniel in a night vision. Therefore Daniel came and stood before the king and said, "Sire, the heavenly powers reveal secrets and make known to the king that which shall come to pass in later days. Thou, O king, sawest a great image whose brightness was excellent and whose form was terrible. The head of this image was of fine gold; breast and arms were of silver; belly and thighs, of brass; legs, of iron; and feet, part of iron and part of clay. A stone smote the feet and broke them to pieces. Then the whole image broke into bits, became like chaff, and the wind carried it away. The stone became a great mountain and filled the earth.

"This was the dream, O King, and this is the interpretation thereof.

"Thou art a king of kings, with power, strength and glory. Thou art this head of gold. After thee shall arise another kingdom, inferior to thine, then a third kingdom of brass which shall bear rule over all the earth. The fourth kingdom shall be as iron but it will break up. The feet, of part iron and part clay, are a sign that the kingdom shall be divided. The great stone is the new kingdom of heaven which shall never be destroyed."

When Daniel had spoken thus, King Nebuchadnezzar honoured him exceedingly and commanded that an oblation and sweet odours be offered him.

He made Daniel a great man. He appointed him ruler over the whole province of Babylon and chief of the governors over all the wise men. At the request of Daniel, his companions, Shadrach, Meshach and Abednego were set over the affairs of the province; and Nebuchadnezzar said to Daniel, "Of a truth your god is the God of gods, Lord of kings, and a revealer of secrets."

THE GOLDEN IMAGE

Nevertheless, King Nebuchadnezzar made an image of gold and set it up in an open space. He sent messengers to gather the people and commanded a herald to make proclamation in these words: "To you it is commanded, O peoples, nations and languages, that at the time you hear the sound of cornet, flute, harp, sackbut, psaltery, dulcimer and all kinds of music, you shall fall down and worship the golden image that Nebuchadnezzar has set up; and whosoever falls not down and worships, he shall that same hour be cast into the midst of a burning fiery furnace."

114

Then was the music sounded and the people worshipped, but certain Chaldeans came to the king and said, "O King, live forever. There are certain Jews—Shadrach, Meshach, and Abednego—who have not regarded the king's decree. They have not worshipped the golden image that thou hast set up."

THE FIERY FURNACE

Nebuchadnezzar, in his rage and fury, commanded that these men be brought before him and he asked, "Is it true, O Shadrach, Meshach, and Abednego, that you do not serve my gods and worship the golden image that I have set up? Know you not that if you worship not, you shall be cast into the midst of the burning fiery furnace?"

Shadrach, Meshach, and Abednego answered, "O King, our god is able to deliver us from the burning fiery furnace and he will surely deliver us out of thy hand; but if not, we still will not worship the golden image which thou hast set up."

Then was Nebuchadnezzar even more full of fury and commanded that the furnace be heated seven times more than was wont. He commanded the most mighty men of his army to bind Shadrach, Meshach, and Abednego in their coats, their hosen, their hats and their other garments and to cast them into the fire.

Because the fire was so hot, it slew those men who took the three, and these three fell down bound into the midst of the burning fiery furnace.

Nebuchadnezzar then looked into the fire and was astonished exceedingly. He said to his counsellors, "Did we not cast three men, bound, into the midst of the fiery furnace? but lo, I see four men, loose, walking in the midst of the fire. They have no hurt and the form of the fourth is like unto an angel."

Then Nebuchadnezzar called to Shadrach, Meshach, and Abednego to come forth and they came forth from the midst of the fire. All the people assembled there looked at them and saw that not a hair of their head was singed, neither were their garments burned nor had the smell of fire passed on to them. The king spoke and said, "Blessed be the god of Shadrach, Meshach, and Abednego, who hath sent his angel to deliver them and hath changed the king's word. I now decree that anyone who speaks anything against their god shall be cut into pieces, for there is no other god that can deliver after this sort," and the king promoted Shadrach, Meshach, and Abednego.

DANIEL INTERPRETS THE KING'S SECOND DREAM

Nebuchadnezzar had a second dream. He dreamed of a great tree in the midst of the earth. The leaves were fair and the fruit was food for all. Then came a holy one down from heaven and said, "Hew down the tree but leave a stump in the earth. Beasts shall roam over it but the stump shall sprout again. This is by decree of the holy ones."

Daniel came to interpret the dream but was troubled in his heart until the king told him to declare the meaning and fear not.

So Daniel said, "The tree, O King, is thou, who art strong and providest for all. Thou shalt be driven from men and live with the beasts, yet shall thy kingdom be sure to thee when thou acknowledgest that the Most High rules in heaven."

As Daniel had said, so it came to pass. The king was driven from his kingdom, but after a season he lifted his eyes to heaven and his reason returned. Then was he established in his kingdom as if new born.

THE WRITING ON THE WALL

When Nebuchadnezzar died, Belshazzar became king. He made a great feast and commanded that the gold and silver vessels which had been taken from the temple in Jerusalem should be used as drinking cups. The king, his wives, the princes, and all the guests, drank from the sacred cups but they praised other gods, gods of gold, of silver, of brass, iron, wood, and stone.

In that same hour came forth fingers of a man's hand and wrote upon the wall of the king's palace. When the king saw it, his countenance was changed, his thoughts troubled him, his joints were loosed, and his knees smote one against another. He cried aloud to bring in the astrologers and the soothsayers and he entreated them: "Whoever shall read this writing and show me the interpretation thereof shall be clothed with scarlet, have a chain of gold about his neck, and he shall be the third ruler in the kingdom."

Then came in all the king's wise men but they could neither read the writing nor interpret it and Belshazzar was greatly troubled. Howbeit, the queen knew of the wisdom of Daniel and he was sent for and brought before the king.

Belshazzar addressed Daniel, saying: "I have heard of thee, that the spirit of the gods is in thee and that light and understanding and excellent wisdom is found in thee. I pray thee, read this writing, show me the interpretation thereof and I will reward thee."

Daniel answered, "Reward I neither desire nor accept, yet I will read the writing and make known the interpretation. O Belshazzar, thou knowest that thy father was great and powerful, yet he humbled himself to possess the kingdom, but thou hast not humbled thy heart. Therefore is this message sent to thee: Mene, Mene, Tekel, Upharsin. This is the meaning:

Mene, Mene: Thy kingdom is coming to an end.

Tekel: Thou art weighed in the balance and found wanting.

Upharsin: Thy kingdom will be divided between the Medes and the Persians."

Then Belshazzar commanded that Daniel be clothed with scarlet, that a chain of gold be put about his neck, and he decreed that Daniel should be the third ruler in the kingdom.

That self-same night was Belshazzar slain and Darius the Median took the kingdom.

A PLOT AGAINST DANIEL

Now Darius saw that there was an excellent spirit in Daniel and thought to set him over the whole realm but other officers and servants of the king were envious. They sought to find fault in him that they might accuse him before the king. They considered among themselves and said, "We shall not find any occasion against this Daniel except we find it concerning the law of his god." So they came before the king and spoke thus: "King Darius, live forever. All the princes, governors, counsellors, and captains have consulted together to ask a royal decree that whosoever shall make a petition to any god or man but thee for thirty days shall be cast into the den of lions." Darius, not knowing what they had in mind, signed the writing and the decree.

When Daniel knew that the writing was signed, he went into his house. He opened his windows towards Jerusalem and he kneeled upon his knees, prayed, and gave thanks before his god as he did aforetime.

Then his enemies assembled and found Daniel praying before his god. They came before the king and said, "That Daniel, of the children of the captivity of Judah, takes no regard of thee nor thy decree but makes prayer to his god three times daily." The king heard these words and was sore displeased with himself. He set his heart on Daniel to deliver him but the assembled men said to him, "O Darius, thou hast made decree. The king's decree is law to everyone."

Thus was Darius constrained to command that Daniel be brought before him and he said, "Thou servant of heaven and of me, thy king, I have made decree which must be obeyed; yet thy god, whom thou servest continually, will surely protect and deliver thee."

Then was Daniel cast into the den of lions.

DANIEL IN THE DEN OF LIONS

The king was troubled. He passed the night fasting and his sleep went from him. In the morning he rose very early and went in haste to the den of lions. As he came there he cried: "Daniel, O Daniel, is thy god able to deliver thee from the lions?" and Daniel answered, "O King, live forever. My god has sent his angel and has shut the lions' mouths."

Then was the king exceeding glad for him and commanded that he be brought up out of the den, and no manner of hurt was found upon him.

Moreover, the king commanded that those men who had sought to ensnare Daniel and bring harm upon him should themselves be cast to the lions; and he then made proclamation throughout his kingdom that men should pay respect to the god of Daniel.

So Daniel prospered in the reign of Darius and also in the reign of Cyrus the Persian who succeeded to the throne.

DANIEL'S VISIONS

In the first year of the reign of Belshazzar Daniel had a vision by night and he saw four beasts coming up out of the sea. The first was like a lion with eagle's wings but the wings were plucked and the beast was made to stand upon its feet. The second beast was a bear who was told to devour much flesh. The third was a leopard with four wings and four heads and the fourth was the most dreadful and terrible. This monster had iron teeth and desired to devour the earth. For a time these beasts had dominion over the earth.

Then Daniel saw one come like the Son of Man with the clouds of heaven. To him was given dominion, glory, and a kingdom, that all people, nations and languages should serve him. His dominion was to be everlasting and not to be destroyed. Daniel became aware of a bystander in his vision and he asked him the meaning of what he saw. The man answered that the beasts were evil beings, enemies of human beings, who would seek to destroy them but that help would come from the Most High in heaven.

In another vision Daniel saw a ram with two horns, one higher than the other; and the ram was pushing its way west, north, south, and nothing could stand against it. Then a he-goat came from the west, with a horn between its eyes. The he-goat attacked the ram, broke his horns and stamped upon him. He drew down stars from heaven and stamped upon them also.

Then the angel Gabriel appeared and said, "The ram with the two horns is the king of Media and Persia. The goat is the king of Grecia. The king of Grecia will overcome the king of Media and Persia and will become great. Those who come after him will destroy holy things."

Daniel had a further vision. He set it down in writing thus: "Then I lifted up mine eyes and looked, and behold, I saw a certain man clothed in linen, whose loins were girded with fine gold. His body was like the beryl and his face as the appearance of lightning, and his eyes as lamps of fire. His arms and his feet were like unto polished brass, and the voice of his words was like the voice of a multitude. He said, 'Fear not, I am come to make thee understand what shall befall thy people in the latter days. In north, and south, and east, and west, there will be wars and an abomination of desolation. From the west will come forth people who make themselves gods and thy people will be delivered up to them, yet in that hour I will be with you.'"

Daniel looked again and there stood the man in linen on the far bank of a river, and on this side was the Archangel Michael, beckoning and pointing to the man in linen. Daniel heard Michael ask: "How long shall it be to the end of these wonders?" and the man answered, "When the time is come."

THE STORY OF ESTHER

Jews are saved from destruction

ESTHER BECOMES QUEEN

Now it came to pass in the days of Ahasuerus (this is Ahasuerus who reigned from India to Ethiopia over one hundred and twenty seven provinces) that in the third year of his reign, in his palace at Shushan, he made a great feast for all his princes, nobles, and servants. To his guests from Media and Persia, to the governors of his provinces, to his nobles, he showed the riches of his glorious kingdom. The court of his palace was adorned with fine hangings, white, green, and blue, fastened with cords of fine linen to silver rings on marble pillars. Couches were of gold and silver, set on a pavement of red, blue and white marble. The guests drank the royal wine from vessels of gold (the vessels all being diverse from one another) and the king commanded that no one should be compelled to drink, but that the officers of his house should do according to every man's pleasure.

Vashti, the queen, made a feast for the women in the royal house.

Now when the heart of the king was merry with wine, he commanded the seven chamberlains to bring Queen Vashti before him that he might show her beauty to the people, for she was fair to look upon. But Queen Vashti refused to come. Therefore was the king very wroth and his anger burned within him. He turned to the wise men at his court and asked, "What shall be done unto the queen according to the law since she has not obeyed the commandment of the king?" The chief of the wise men answered, "Queen Vashti has not only done wrong against the king but by her example has encouraged other women to despise their husbands. Therefore shall Vashti come no more before the king and her royal state shall be given to another. Let fair young maidens be sought out and brought before the king and let the maiden that best pleases him be made queen."

This judgement pleased the king. Vashti came no more before him and search was made for a fair young maiden to replace her.

Now there was a certain Jew in the king's service whose name was Mordecai and he had brought up his uncle's daughter, Esther, because both her father and her mother were dead. She was fair and beautiful and came with other maidens into the king's house, saying nothing of her people or kindred. This maiden pleased the king above all others and he took her for his queen and made a great feast.

CONSPIRACY TO MURDER THE KING

In those days two of the king's chamberlains plotted to slay King Ahasuerus but the thing became known to Mordecai. He reported it to Esther and Esther certified it to the king in Mordecai's name. When inquisition was made of the matter, it was found to be true and the two conspirators were hanged on a tree and this event was recorded in the book of Chronicles.

Also in the king's service was a man called Haman who had found great favor in the king's eyes and whom the king promoted. The king commanded that all the servants in the palace should bow to him and reverence him. Howbeit, Mordecai bowed not and he told certain of the servants that he was a Jew.

PLOT AGAINST THE JEWS

When Mordecai bowed not to him, Haman was full of wrath, and when it came to his ears that Mordecai was a Jew, he resolved on a way to destroy him and all the Jews in the kingdom whom he liked not. He said to King Ahasuerus, "There are a certain people scattered throughout thy kingdom whose laws are different from the king's laws. They are a danger to thy kingdom. Therefore let it be decreed that they be destroyed."

The king trusted Haman and gave him his ring, saying, "Do with them as seems good to thee."

Then Haman commanded the scribes to write to all the governors of all the provinces that, on a certain day, all Jews, young and old, be put to death and he sealed the letters with the seal of the king's ring.

This same proclamation was also made in Shushan and the inhabitants of the city were sore perplexed. Throughout all the cities of the land there was great mourning, fasting, weeping and wailing among the Jews. When the tidings were brought to Mordecai, he rent his clothes and cried with a loud and bitter cry.

Esther's maids told her what had come to pass and she grieved exceedingly. She called one of the king's chamberlains and despatched him to Mordecai to seek advice, to say also, "It is the law that whosoever shall come unto the king in the inner court who is not called shall be put to death unless the king hold out the golden sceptre. I have not been called these thirty days."

ESTHER INTERCEDES

Mordecai made answer, saying, "Fear not. Go unto the king in the inner court and make plea for thy people. Who knows whether thou art become queen for such a time as this."

So Esther went and stood in the inner court of the king's house and the king held out his sceptre towards her, asking, "What wilt thou, Queen Esther? It shall be given thee, even unto the half of my kingdom."

Esther answered, "If I have found favor in the sight of the king, and if it please him, let the king and Haman come to a banquet that I will prepare for them; then shall my request be made known to thee."

That day Haman went forth with a glad heart. He boasted of his riches, of the manner in which the king had promoted him, of his invitation to Esther's banquet with the king alone.

On that night the king could not sleep. He commanded that the book of Chronicles be brought and read to him. It was found written that Mordecai had prevented the king's murder and the king asked, "What honour or reward did Mordecai receive for this service?" and the servants answered, "Nothing was done for him." Then said the king, "Is anyone in the court?"

The servants looked and lo, there was Haman, come to petition the king to hang Mordecai for disobedience, for which task he had already prepared a gallows.

So Haman came before the king and at once the king asked, "What should be done unto the man whom the king delights to honour?" Then Haman thought in his heart, "The king desires to honour me," and he answered, "Let royal apparel be brought, also the horse on which the king rides, and a crown. Let the man be arrayed with a crown and the royal apparel and let him be brought on horseback through the city. Let his worth be proclaimed before him."

Then the king said to Haman, "Thy words are good. Make haste, take apparel and horse as thou hast said, and do even as thou hast spoken to Mordecai, for I am indebted to him."

Haman did as the king bade but with mourning and a bitter heart.

The next day, the king and Haman attended the banquet to which Esther had invited them and the king said, "Make known thy request, Queen Esther. It shall be granted thee, even unto the half of my kingdom."

Then Esther spoke, saying, "O King, if I have found favor in thy sight, let my life be given me and let the lives of the Jews, my people, be given them for we are to be put to death, to be slain, for no just reason."

At these words King Ahasueras was exceedingly astonished and asked, "Who is he who hath made this unjust charge and condemnation?" and Esther answered, "The adversary and enemy is this wicked Haman who sits here beside thee."

JUSTICE IS DONE

Then one of the king's servants stood before him and reported that Haman had prepared a gallows for Mordecai. When the king heard these things, he arose in his wrath, saying, "Take Haman and hang him on the gallows he has prepared." So Haman was hanged and the king's wrath was assuaged.

The king advanced Mordecai into the place of Haman and at once the scribes were ordered to write letters to the governors to reverse the order of Haman to destroy the Jews. Moreover, the king looked favorably upon them and many people of other nations came unto their beliefs.

As for Mordecai, not only was he great among his own people and brethren but he became next to Ahasuerus in the kingdom.

THE RETURN TO JERUSALEM:
EZRA, NEHEMIAH

Reform and reconstruction

THE EMPEROR SENDS A PARTY OF JEWS TO JERUSALEM TO REBUILD THE TEMPLE

The Emperor, Cyrus, was well disposed towards the Jews and Jehovah stirred up his spirit that he made a proclamation throughout all his kingdom and put it also in writing thus: "Jehovah Elohim has given me all the kingdoms of the earth and he has charged me to build him a house at Jerusalem which is in Judah. Therefore if any of his people desire, let such go up to Jerusalem and build the house of the god of Israel."

Then the elders of Judah rose up. They were given vessels of silver and gold, goods, beasts, and precious things. Also Cyrus brought forth the vessels of the temple which Nebuchadnezzar had taken and gave them to them.

So all Jews who wished to return were granted leave and they came to Jerusalem to rebuild the temple. In the second year of their coming the foundations were laid and the people sang together in praise and thanks and shouted with a great shout.

MORE JEWS RETURN

When Artaxerxes became king, he appointed Ezra, a priest and scribe of holy law, to lead more Jews back to Judah. Artaxerxes also allowed one of his servants, Nehemiah, to return, for Nehemiah had told him that he wished to help to rebuild the wall of the city of Jerusalem. Not only did Artaxerxes give him leave but he also commanded the keeper of the king's forests to provide Nehemiah with timber for rebuilding the city gates.

Nehemiah became governor of Judah and Ezra, a priest and a scribe, wrote down the laws of Jehovah and taught them to the people.

126

THE TWELVE MINOR PROPHETS

Besides the famous prophets already mentioned, there were many others.

Amos lived in the eighth century B.C. at about the same time as Isaiah. He was a native of the mountains of Judah and was inspired to go to the northern kingdom to denounce the ungodly state of affairs there and to call for a change of ways. He also preached about the wicked ways of other nations.

Hosea, Micah, Zephaniah, Obadiah, Joel, all called for a better way of living and looked forward to the coming of the Messiah.

Nahum directed his words to Nineveh, Habbakuk to the Chaldeans (Babylonians).

The prophets Haggai and Zechariah were active in Jerusalem as the first Jews returned to build the temple in the Cyrus period. Little notice was taken of them.

The last book of the Old Testament is entitled Malachi, which is not a name but means *my messenger*. The writer complained of the Israelites' ingratitude towards their god, of their wicked ways and the fact that their priests neglected their duties. He prophesied divine judgement on the wicked and divine blessing on the good. He looked forward to the day of Christ's coming and announced that a great prophet would prepare his way.

BOOKS BY ROY WILKINSON

Questions and Answers on Rudolf Steiner Education
The Temperaments in Education
The Interpretation of Fairy Tales
The Curriculum of the Rudolf Steiner School
Commonsense Schooling
Rudolf Steiner on Education

Wilkinson Waldorf Curriculum Series:
Teaching English
Teaching Mathematics
Teaching Physics and Chemistry
Teaching Geography
Teaching History I: *Ancient Civilizations, Greece, Rome*
Teaching History II: *Middle Ages, Renaissance to Second World War*
Old Testament Stories
Commentary on the Old Testament Stories
The Norse Stories and Their Significance
Teaching Practical Activities: *Farming, Gardening, Housebuilding*
The Human Being and the Animal World
Plant Study and Geology
Nutrition, Health, and Anthropology
Miscellany: *A Collection of Poems and Plays*
Plays for Puppets

The Origin and Development of Language
The Spiritual Basis of Rudolf Steiner Education

Rudolf Steiner: Aspects of his spiritual world view (3 volumes)
Anthroposophy vol. I: *Rudolf Steiner. Reincarnation and karma. The spiritual nature of the human being. The development of human consciousness.*
Anthroposophy vol. II: *Evolution of the world and humanity. Relationships between the living and the dead. Forces of evil. The modern path of initiation.*
Anthroposophy vol. III: *Life between death and rebirth. The spiritual hierarchies. The philosophical approach to the spirit. The mission of Christ.*

May be ordered from: Rudolf Steiner College Bookstore
9200 Fair Oaks Boulevard
Fair Oaks, CA 95628, U.S.A.
E-mail: steinercollege.edu Tel: (916) 961-8729 — Fax: (916) 961-3032